PHOTOGRAPHY
DAVID LEVENSON
TEXT
TREVOR HALL

First published in Great Britain 1984 by Colour Library Books Ltd.
© 1984 Illustrations and text: Colour Library Books Ltd.,
    Guildford, Surrey, England.
Display and text filmsetting by Acesetters Ltd.,
    Richmond, Surrey, England.
Colour separations by Llovet, S.A., Barcelona, Spain.
Printed and bound in Barcelona, Spain by Rieusset and Gráficas Estella.
ISBN 0 86283 253 5

IN CELEBRATION
of The
QUEEN'S Visit to CANADA

COLOUR LIBRARY BOOKS

Everyone enjoys a birthday party, and the Canada the Queen and Prince Philip visited in September and October 1984 was awash with them. Only the most courageous commentator will venture to specify the precise date when a country achieves real nationhood – in Canada's case, you have a choice of several dates from 1837 to 1982 – but you could never deny that this expansive former dominion is already proud and festive about the momentous events in its comparatively short and almost precociously swift rise to statehood. That was well proved by this latest of royal tours, which became a progress to celebrate everything from the major centenaries of great provinces and cities to the lesser anniversaries of parishes and local institutions.

It was only natural that the Queen should be invited to join in these festivities. No other country has hosted her so frequently – this was her fourteenth visit since her accession – and among no other of her former colonial subjects does she feel more evidently at home. If it was ever difficult to detect the root cause of this patently pleasurable mutuality, this two-week early-Autumn visit explained it all in letters writ large and vivid. For the people of New Brunswick and Ontario in particular, loyalty to the Crown and an almost personal affection for Queen Elizabeth II have become part of the way of life. The devotional tradition goes way back to the days of the American Revolution, when those who chose to remain supportive of the British Crown fled from Vermont, Maine and New York State to set up communes across the eastern lakes or on the northern banks of the St Lawrence. Their new life-style was staunchly defended three decades later, when the threat of an American invasion loomed dark and very real. The loyalties which prompted such embattled determination were specifically applauded by the present Prince of Wales during his visit in 1983, when he expressed 'the belated thanks of His Late Majesty King George III for your unswerving loyalty and devotion to the Crown.' And it was these same mutual sentiments that brought the Queen to those provinces, and subsequently to Manitoba, as a distinguished guest and fellow celebrant, rather than as a visitor imposed upon a submissive colony by the paid representatives of the Mother Country.

It has long been a source of pride among Canadians that they should put on the very best of

shows for the Queen and her consort, and some acts in the course of past tours have been difficult to better. But this year's programme was no disappointment to the royal guests, and certainly no disgrace to hosts who almost tumbled over each other to provide the most spectacular entertainment, the most absorbing cultural displays, the most generous demonstrations of personal esteem, and the most colourful evidence of the spirit of celebration which pervaded the entire, busy, bustling fortnight. You would be forgiven for imagining that in no country but Canada could you witness a microcosm of Italian culture on one day, and of Ukrainian traditions only shortly afterwards; or an exhibition of native Indian life almost cheek by jowl with one of European elegance in fashion; or the faithfully recreated ritual of loyalist warfare on the same day as reconstructions of Indian landings in previously unexplored territory.

More routine, less colourful work for the Queen was sandwiched between these localised delights – a reminder, perhaps, that whatever the attractions of the past, today is with us and tommorrow lies before us in outward garb less beguiling than the romantic memories of years gone by. But it was a tonic to feel that Canadians can resolve the awkward equation of making room for the past in such a way as to give meaning to the present and – who knows? – a sense of direction, or at least of balance, as they face the future. It was this theme that the Queen returned to again and again, which is partly why it made such good sense to have her back among her Canadian subjects once more. As Queen of Canada, she likes to be associated with Canadians in whatever way they feel she can be of most help. It is no longer inconvenient for her to be brought over from Britain year after year, and she has willingly and sympathetically adapted to the necessity of regular and frequent visits to her subjects over the water – a necessity which was certainly not considered to exist in the days of her great-great-grandmother.

Before the mid-19th century, official visits abroad were rarely a feature of royal life – and in this respect the British Royal Family was no different from its European counterparts. Even the spasmodic visits to Canada of King George III's fourth son, Edward Duke of Kent, whilst on naval duties in the early 1790s, were little more than courtesy calls, paid to give the Mother Country's Dominion representatives the occasional chance to ingratiate themselves with their sovereign. It was the Duke of Kent's grandson – Albert Edward, Prince of Wales – to whom is credited the pioneering spirit of becoming a royal ambassador to Empire, and it was Canada that secured his first official foreign tour in 1860. His mother, Queen Victoria, was reluctant with her permission. She had refused an invitation to visit Canada herself, for fear of the dangers and fatigue of a long voyage, and it was only in recognition of Canadian loyalty in sending a regiment to join the British troops in the Crimea in 1856 that impelled her to offer her son and heir as her delegate. Most politicians were sceptical of the value of the Prince's prospective journey, and the Colonial Office was particularly unenthusiastic. But Prince Albert, not to mention *The Times*, was convinced that there was mileage to be made from 'the useful cooperation of the Royal Family in the civilisation which England developed and advanced.' But for the Prince of Wales, it was a liberating alternative to a dull diet of filial duty and academic study, and he seized the opportunity for this new-found freedom with glee.

He may not have found the outward voyage much to his liking, over-full as it was of studying maps and memorising constitutional details, but once in Canada he never looked back, despite pouring rain which dogged much of his time there. Everything came alive with his entry into Halifax, Nova Scotia, where stores closed down for two days, and even newspapers failed to appear. From then until the end of his two-month stay, his schedule was packed with processions, levées, banquets, audiences and endless addresses of welcome. He sent frequent letters – dutifully factual, though rarely descriptive – back home, enclosing with one of them a piece of sweet briar from the derelict remains of the Duke of Kent's Lodge, which his grandfather had occupied almost seventy years before. Meanwhile, the Duke of Newcastle, charged by Queen Victoria and Prince Albert to keep a fatherly eye on the errant son's doings, was able to report how impressed the Canadians were with the Prince's manner – 'frank and friendly, without any mixture of assumed study to gain popularity by over-civility.' Clearly his *forte* was his personality, which never prospered better than at the all-night balls staged in his honour. At the Mayor's Ball in Quebec, he was on the dance-floor throughout the night, taking part in every one of the twenty-two dances. At Montreal, too, he refused to sit out a single

dance in that famous and extravagant ballroom with its fountains running with claret and champagne, and its superb gardens with their artificial, illuminated lakes. Every woman fell for his charm, and he encouraged their blind devotion. At a ball in Hamilton, he exchanged mischievous whispers with them with such abandon that the *New York Herald* was convinced that he 'looks as if he might have a very susceptible nature, and has already yielded to several twinges in the region of his midriff.'

News of his affable behaviour preceded him everywhere, and even affected the sometimes delicate politics of the times. To his triumphant entry into Quebec was imputed an almost miraculous cooling of hostility between French and British sympathisers. At Kingston, the Orangemen, faced with the Prince's refusal to land unless they removed their Orange arches and played down the sectarian tenor of their prospective welcome, defied the Prince by drafting a drunken resolution inviting the him 'to land and be decorated with Orange orders, or to go to hell and take his flunkeys with him.' Then, two days later, they turned up at Toronto and, full of apologies, this delegation of confident, grown men tearfully begged the forgiveness of this 18-year-old boy. Elsewhere, the sense of fun for which his own grandson, the future King Edward VIII, was to become equally, if not better known, captivated the Canadians. He shot the St. Lawrence rapids on a raft, and even volunteered to be wheeled by Blondin across the Niagara Falls on a tightrope, until the Duke of Newcastle prevented him. His hosts could not do enough for him. The Falls were illuminated in his honour, Indian tribes emerged everywhere to greet him, and his comings and goings spawned a host of advertisements which used his name to peddle everything from umbrellas to cans of beans. It was a hugely successful personal visit, though the Duke of Newcastle saw a longer-term benefit. He told Queen Victoria that the future would demonstrate 'the good that has been done. The attachment to the Crown of England has been greatly cemented, and other nations have learned how useless it will be in case of war to tamper with the allegiance of the North American province.'

In those circumstances, it was a shame that the Prince never returned to Canada. Even as King, he found a convenient excuse for refusing an invitation to visit the country for Quebec's tercentenary in 1908, despite an unctuous plea to 'allow Canadians to express their profound admiration for those kingly virtues and truly humanitarian deeds which have earned Your Majesty the first place amongst the great sovereigns of the world.' Concealing the fact that he was a European at heart, he pleaded the necessity of being within call of England, and sent his son, the future King George V, to Canada instead. It turned out to be a happy substitution. Despite his innate conservatism, the then Prince of Wales was careful to avoid patronising the understandably sensitive French Canadians, taking especial pains not to exclude mention of the French contribution to Canada's history. At Wolfe's Monument, he spoke emphatically of 'the historic battlefields of Quebec, on which two contending races won equal and imperishable glory.' And throughout the week-long visit, he pioneered the now traditional royal formula of speaking to the Quebecois in French as well as English. 'The Prince of Wales has taught the people of Quebec how to cheer wrote the Governor-General, as the visit came to a close, and even the Prince himself reflected gratefully that relations between English and French Canadians had never been better. He was thrilled to be able to present a cheque for £90,000, representing Empire-wide donations for the acquisition by the Canadian people of the Quebec battlefields, as no doubt his wife was thrilled by at least one of the gifts he took back for her – a mink coat with 24-carat gold buttons, presented to him by the people of Nova Scotia.

The Prince of Wales had, as Duke of York, already paid a major official visit to Canada in the autum of 1901, part of a monumental eight-month tour of the Empire, which had been proposed as early as 1898, but delayed so that the first Australian Federal Parliament could be opened in State in mid-1901. The North American stage of the tour was also the final one but, then as now, exuberance was the hallmark of the Canadian welcome, just as the most unpleasant of weather had become a feature of royal arrivals there. Fog, then rain, hampered the Duke and Duchess' vessel *HMS Ophir* on its progress up the St. Lawrence, and a squally wind turned into a frightening storm as she dropped anchor at Quebec. But there were huge crowds to greet them, the blaze of bunting in harbour and streets mirrored by the overall dressing of warships – tempered though this was by the half-masted

American flag in memory of the recently assassinated President McKinley. A spectacular firework display, staged that evening before an illuminated Fleet, was marred when one tug's consignment of fireworks blew up prematurely, setting the whole craft instantly ablaze, and sending explosions rocketing off in all directions. Visiting, as he was, in the middle of the Boer War, the Duke – then on his third trip to Quebec – took care to thank the Canadians for their contribution to the war effort, deftly shielding the reality of that conflict's cost in human life behind the hope that 'the blood shed on battlefields in South Africa may, like that shed by your fathers in 1775 and 1812, weave fresh strands in the cord of brotherhood that binds together our glorious Empire.'

That sentiment grates today, so it is good – even somewhat surprising – to know that the Duke, as a young man at least, was capable of more perceptive, less hidebound reactions to events and situations. At Ottawa, he described the Federation of Canada as pre-eminent among the political events of the nineteenth century. At Regina, he vividly contrasted the 'free, healthy and useful life' of the area with the 'narrow and alas! too often unwholesome existence of the thousands in our great cities at home', and he repeated this theme on his return to London when, in his famous 'Wake Up, England!' speech at the Guildhall, he called for more emigration to take advantage of opportunities in the Colonies. At Calgary, he marshalled all his diplomatic tact to reply to the Alberta Indians in their own parlance, speaking of Queen Victoria as 'The Great Mother', of earlier years of troubles as 'days when your pipes were cold, your tents melancholy', and giving assurances that 'my Great Father the King's promises will last as long as sun shall shine and waters shall flow.'

The welcome the Indians gave him was arguably the most colourful – certainly the most unusual – of the tour, for here the self-conscious and elegantly-dressed royal party was surrounded by Indians, many of whom were almost completely naked, coated only in war-paint, and sporting great plumes and feathes. One horseman attracted much attention when he appeared totally covered with yellow paint, save for a few daubs of vermilion on his face, and riding a horse streaked with yellow ochre and decorated with feathers. But there was no doubting the sincerity of the welcome. Presenting a copy of the treaty of 1874 whereby the Indians had ceded their independence to Queen Victoria, they expressed their gratitude, to 'the Great Spirit for this occasion' and for the opportunity of meeting 'the illustrious grandson of Her Late Majesty Queen Victoria, whose death we most deeply lament'. The Duke presented each Chief with a medal struck on King Edward's orders, to be worn on all ceremonial occasions by them and by their successors.

The tour took the Duke and Duchess from the East to the extreme West of Canada – Vancouver and Victoria were the most westerly stops – and back again via the Niagara Falls. We are reliably told that they shook hands with 35,000 people, gave almost a hundred speeches, and distributed 140 titles. The Duke also took time off to shoot game while in the West, and sent a moose head to *HMS Ophir* to be packed ready for the voyage back to England. The *Ophir*, after a thorough clean in dry dock, was waiting for the royal party in Halifax, her pristine white hull trimmed with blue, and her buff-coloured, enamel-coated funnels shining in the late autum sun. Halifax itself was speckled with bunting and flags, and a sizeable crowd saw the Duke and Duchess off, including a large party of Indians – 'most of them in full savage dress', as one crew-member observed – who had travelled hundreds of miles to see the royal couple arrive at Halifax by train and leave again by sea. Snow impeded progress towards Newfoundland, and the *Ophir* had to negotiate icebergs as well as the narrow harbour entrance at St John's for a brief call. Bonfires crackled on high ground, and the message 'Welcome to Terra Nova' was painted on the coastal headland. And, never short of imaginative ideas, their hosts sent the royal couple off with a nine-month-old Newfoundland dog harnessed to a mail-cart, as a present for their seven-year-old son, Prince Edward. Small wonder that, in his farewell letter to the Governor-General, the Duke spoke of his 'imperishable memories of affectionate and loyal hearts, frank and independent natures, prosperous and progressive communities, boundless productive territories, glorious scenery, stupendous works of nature, and a people and country proud of their membership of the Empire, and in which the Empire finds one of its brightest offspring.

The future King George V's own offspring paid several visits to Canada in their turn, and the first and most famous of these visits was that paid by his eldest, Edward Prince of Wales, in 1919. Conceived as the first of several grand Empire tours, it was one of four he made to Canada, two of which, though each lasting well over a month, were unofficial. The Prince was twenty-five years of age when he first set foot in the Dominion, and his less than biddable behaviour *vis-à-vis* his parents prompted the King, like Prince Albert before him, to add an older, 'Establishment' figure (this time in the shape of Rear-Admiral Sir Lionel Halsey) to his son's retinue. It was illustrative of the relationship between father and son that the Prince was less inclined to the King's stolid, Victorian concept of the tour than to Lloyd George's vision of it as a 'first-class carnival' in which the Prince should display 'a many-sided and natural role'. The former ideal certainly materialised in the endless programme of State drives, mounted military parades, civic lunches and after-dinner speeches, all of which soon made it clear to the Prince that, unless he changed matters, the tour would be run very much in line with his father's 1901 visit. But in the event, any pretensions to pomposity were soon exposed when, on his arrival at St John's, Newfoundland, he noticed that the triumphal arch under which he walked in procession was built of drums containing cod-liver oil, and festooned with dried fish carcases! This somewhat irreverent observation, and the amazing but enjoyable discovery of the effusive vigour of volatile crowds in Quebec made him realise that a novel and more original royal response was required. Amused, if faintly alarmed, by the way the Quebecois repeatedly broke through police cordons to snatch at his tie or handkerchief, or to tear his buttons from his coat, he was quick to brush aside his organiser's abject apology – 'I simply cannot understand what has come over the Canadian people, Sir' – and made a straight-forward but ardent plea for a revision of the arrangements in favour of a less formal programme. The request was resisted until, at the Toronto Exhibition Grounds, a horseback review of those who had just come back from the War turned into a scrummage as the cheering veterans suddenly broke ranks, surged round the Prince, lifted him from his horse, and passed him, like a football, over their heads till he eventually reached the dais. Thenceforth, formality was kept to a minimum. It was in Toronto, too, that a chance remark by one war veteran during a presentation – 'Put it there, Ed: I shook hands with your grand-dad' – led the Prince to make himself available at all future events to meet anybody who cared to come up and shake hands with him. But that plan backfired. Time constraints made it necessary to call a halt on successive occasions, and in any case it took only a week for the Prince's right hand to become so black, swollen and painful from the continued enthusiastic handshaking that, in his own words, he 'retired it temporarily from Imperial service, and offered the left instead.'

Thirty years later, as Duke of Windsor, he was to describe that tour as 'the most exhilarating I have ever known', and its tone led him to make significant modifications to the accepted habit of royal speechmaking, as well as contact with the public. At first, he found little difficulty in making the right noises. 'I'm rubbing it in', he told his father, 'that although not actually Canadian-born, I'm a Canadian in spirit, and come over here as such, and not as a stranger – and that goes down well'. That approach had been drilled into him by his mentors, but he himself began to change the emphasis. The CPR train which took him to over fifty towns in three months was fitted with an observation platform so that communities from settlements all along the track could see him. Often their enthusiasm halted the train and he was called upon to speak to loyal groups of spectators. In time, he evolved a convenient, standard three-minute speech, interlaced with useful local facts which had been supplied to him only minutes before by his staff. But he found that, all too frequently, haste led to embarrassing blunders, so he took to the idea of using these enforced halts to get off the train, stretch his legs, and chat informally with the locals, be they miners, farmers, industrial workers, or whoever. This pleasing and popular approach taught him far more about those he had come to visit than anything he could learn in more formal surroundings.

Needless to say, the Canadians responded magnificently to his personal touch, and no-one seemed to enjoy it all more than he.Legends in words and pictures were created during those three months: the report of the war veteran who fought with police to establish his right to meet the Prince personally; the story of how, when the cap of a wounded chair-bound soldier was whisked off by the wind, the Prince sprinted after it, retrieved it, and placed it back on its owner's head; the enduring photograph of the sailor Prince signing an official Visitors' Book, with a cigarette cocked jauntily between his lips; another picture of him resplendent in the full feathered head-dress of an Indian Chief; the experience of seeing him graduate from spectator to performer at an exhibition of bronco-busting at Saskatoon, where he acquitted himself by staying the full course. He joined a cattle round-up at the Bar U Ranch in Alberta, went duck-shooting at the Qu'Appelle Lake in Saskatchewan, and spent a few days at an Indian camp near the Nipigon river, eating Indian food, canoeing, and fishing for trout. Not surprisingly, it was here that he declared that, for a real holiday, Canada would be his first choice, and the thought impelled him to buy 1,600 acres, and lease a further 2,400, of land at Pekisko High River, seventy miles south of Calgary, which, in deference to his own formal initials, he called the EP Ranch. Here he reared pedigree cattle, ponies and sheep, creating a successful going concern by 1927; he applied for a licence to work minerals in 1930, and even hoped for an oil-strike in the 1940's. He visited the ranch several times after his abdication, selling in up in 1962 for a reported $190,000.

His second official visit in 1927, made in the company of his youngest surviving brother, the Duke of Kent, and of British Prime Minister Stanley Baldwin, was a shorter and more formal business, involving his attendance at the celebrations marking the Diamond Jubilee of the Confederation, and his inauguration of the Peace Bridge across the Niagara Falls. But the memory of that first, heady visit remained ineradicable for years afterwards. It did much to explain the vacillating attitude of Canada's politicians in 1936, when the abdication issue arose. 'He really is idolised here', wrote the Governor-General, Lord Tweedsmuir, at the time. 'Canada feels that he is her own possession'.

The trauma of the Abdication was well and truly past by the time of the next royal visit to Canada. In 1939, less than three years after their accession, the new King, George VI, and Queen Elizabeth, now the Queen Mother, embarked on an exhausting and comprehensive six-week State Visit there. Following the path of their predecessors, they were taken from coast to coast, and the colour, dazzle and intensity of their reception quickly eclipsed their brilliant State Visit to

France the previous year. The tour was very nearly written off, first because of the political situation in Europe, where constant war alerts made it imperative that their proposed warship transport, *HMS Repulse,* should stay in home waters, and secondly when their substitute liner Empress of Australia almost collided with an iceberg. 'We very nearly hit an iceberg the day before yesterday', the Queen wrote to Queen Mary, 'and the poor Captain was nearly demented because some kind, cheerful people kept reminding him that it was about here that the Titanic was struck – and just about the same date'. The drifting ice floes held them up for some days, but when they berthed safely on 17th May at Quebec, King George achieved the distinction of becoming the first reigning British sovereign to tread on Canadian soil.

The tour was a resounding success. Travel was mostly by means of the 'silver and blue train' as it was familiarly known – a 300-ton blue and aluminium CPR locomotive pulling twelve streamlined coaches over a total of more than 9,000 miles in the course of a 40-day journey from Quebec to Vancouver and back to Halifax. At every station – and with a full programme which left very little time for relaxation, there were *many* stations – there was a crowd to greet the King and Queen. For their part, they had given instructions to be alerted whenever well-wishers were spotted by the side of the railway line, so that their long wait could be properly rewarded. Like most tours, this one had its formal and informal moments. For the Queen, the laying of the foundation stone of the new Supreme Court building in Ottawa was perhaps the most memorable. She mused on the fact that she, and not the King, had been asked to perform the ceremony, but concluded that the choice was appropriate as 'woman's position in modern society has depended upon the growth of law'. Among the more informal interludes was the private visit to see the famous Dionne quins, who had been born in Canada five years earlier. The Queen herself was credited with miraculous powers when, despite persistent rain during a drive through Winnipeg, she instructed that the car roof should be let down so that people could see her. Almost immediately, the rain stopped! But she seemed to have enough personal magic of her own. As one commentator said, 'As for the Queen, she appeared and the day was won. So simple in her bearing and yet so refined, so spontaneous in

every move and yet so harmonious, so radiant with feminine charm and so expressive of emotion, she also found the true words for every occasion and every person'. Lord Tweedsmuir, still Canada's Governor-General, praised the Queen's creditable acquittal of her duties, with the grateful sincerity of of one to whom the organisation of such a massive enterprise proved well worth the effort. 'The Queen has a perfect genius for the right kind of publicity. The unrehearsed episodes were marvellous', he wrote, and he went on to describe how popular she had been for ignoring the set programme, wandering towards the crowds to meet them personally. The royal visitors enjoyed the tour too. 'It made us!' the Queen confided to Canada's Prime Minister Mackenzie King, and she was no doubt pleased that her impeccable French had, as in Paris the previous year, stood her in good stead with the French-speaking communities throughout the country.

Regrettably the King never saw Canada again, but almost three years after his death his widow was back, spending five days in Ottawa. Because of her visit, she was unable to be in London for Prince Charles' sixth birthday, but he was thrilled to receive a trans-Atlantic telephone call from her instead. In June 1962, she went to Montreal to attend the centenary celebrations of the Black Watch (Royal Highland Regiment) of Canada, of which she is still Colonel-in-Chief, and three years later she celebrated the jubilee of the Scottish Regiment in Toronto. A slightly more prolonged visit was arranged in July 1967, when a ten-day programme took her to the Atlantic provinces of New Brunswick, Nova Scotia, Prince Edward Island and Newfoundland. In June 1974 she was back yet again, to present new colours to each of her two regiments in Toronto and Montreal. Four years ago, she paid a seven-day visit to Halifax and Toronto, and in July 1981, attended the bicentennial celebrations of Niagara-on-the-Lake during another week-long visit to Ontario. Though none of her seven visits to Canada in the last three decades has ever equalled the scale and sparkle of that splendidly successful pre-War tour, Canadians are quietly delighted that she has maintained the commitment it engendered, and which she herself expressed at the time with the assurance, 'When I'm in Canada, I am a Canadian.'

After the Second World War, as after the first,

there was a concerted royal effort to do the Empire rounds again, and the King and Queen, accompanied by their two daughters, began the cycle with a long, colourful and triumphal tour of South Africa in 1947. During it, Princess Elizabeth came of age, dedicating herself to the Empire's service for life, and it was she who was chosen to represent the King when in 1951 Canada's turn for another royal tour came round. In the twelve years since her parents' visit the changes were, for the times, remarkable. It was the first royal tour in which the aeroplane played a part, the outward journey from London and several internal connections being made by air. It was also the first in which televised outside broadcasts allowed those Canadians fortunate enough to possess televisions to see the progress of the visit from time to time. Above all, it was the first in which the celebrity was not the monarch or his eldest son, but a young and attractive princess, accompanied by her sporty, personable and good-looking consort. It all combined to make the visit, despite its slavish similarity to those of past years, sufficiently different and lively for it to be a success pretty well from the start. As if to pay special tribute to their hosts, the royal couple's official portraits to mark the tour were taken by the Ottawa photographer, Karsh, and the Princess took with her the full-length mink coat which the people of Canada had given to her on her marriage four years earlier.

For some time the tour was in the balance owing to the King's severe illness which, as we now know, signalled the road to his death four months later. As a result, the Princess and the Duke of Edinburgh left a week behind schedule, and the ceremonial disembarkation planned at Quebec Harbour had to be substituted for muted civilities at Montreal airport. Appropriately, perhaps, they arrived on Thanksgiving Day, though the drizzling rain that greeted them augured ill for their chances with the weather for the next five weeks. Indeed, rain became such a persistent feature that, by the time the tour reached Winnipeg, the organisers had persuaded de Haviland to manufacture a plexiglass car-roof so that the royal couple might be protected from the weather, yet still be visible to the huge crowds who stood in appalling conditions to cheer them. The car's other practical embellishments to this same end were interior lighting from below, and a back-seat heater – but it wasn't the complete answer to the problems of the climate. At Regina,

the first frosts of the tour drove an open-air display by the Mounties indoors, and at a Calgary stampede, seventeen degrees of frost and a blizzard – dismissed contemptuously by the locals as 'just confetti' – had the visitors wrapped in thick electric blankets. Rain soaked the ground so throughly at Vancouver that Press buses, laden with a total of 150 journalists and photographers, were bogged down, and they missed a tree-planting ceremony in which Princess Elizabeth shovelled mud rather than earth onto the sapling's roots. But the royal couple were better prepared for their visit to Niagara Falls: the Duke was fully togged out in black oilskins and rubber boots; the Princess was more elegantly robed in rose-coloured waterproofs.

It is now, and was then, a cliché to talk of adverse weather being incapable of suppressing the popular clamour for royalty, but the truth of that observation was evident during the whole of those hectic five weeks. The 13,000 schoolchildren who sang *O Canada* at Ottawa in the early days turned out to be a comparatively small crowd. There were 40,000 of them to cheer the visitors to the echo at Toronto, and a civic reception at the City Hall became the occasion for chaotic crowd behaviour in which people rushed around everywhere for the best view, clambered up outer walls of buildings, shinned up forbidden lamp-posts and statues, and left the emergency services with no fewer than eighty stretcher cases. Hundreds of Indian children gathered at Fort William, having travelled four hundred miles by canoe from their compounds to see the Princess and her husband. At Montreal, the royal couple made a 75-mile tour of the city's streets by car, passing before an estimated two million people lining the route. From the first week, when all Quebec's church bells sounded their welcoming peals, and when the key to Ottawa was presented to the Princess as representing 'the key to two hundred thousand loyal hearts', neither hosts nor guests could have been in any doubt about the strength of popular feeling for this refreshingly young couple.

In return they were game for most things. They turned up for a square-dance party thrown by the Governor-General in Ottawa — Princess Elizabeth wearing a gingham blouse and swaggering dirndl, while the Duke looked positively rakish in blue jeans, suede loafers, a scarlet neck-tie and a check shirt that, some said, still had the price tag attached! At Calgary, they arrived at the stampede in an old mail-coach — the Halifax, Truro and Pictou — that had ferried the Prince of Wales about in 1860. The Duke, wearing a ten-gallon stetson, was in superb spirits after having joined his wife for a cow-punchers' lunch in a chuck-wagon. The grub-pile included sow-belly, punk and axle-grease, CPR strawberries, and sinkers. Or, in the Queen's English, the menu included boiled pork, bread and butter, prunes and doughnuts. At Edmonton, they watched a football game between the Edmonton Eskimos and the Winnipeg Blue Bombers; at North Bay, Ontario, they met the Dionne quins — now seventeen years old and still world celebrities; and at Victoria the Princess actually drove a locomotive for fifteen miles — with the Duke lending an occasional hand.

There was, of course, a huge amount of rail travel for the royal couple, undertaken in a ten-coach train whose living quarters were decorated in Princess Elizabeth's favourite colour, sea-green. But the Duke didn't take too kindly to the continual train journeys, and found the heating system particularly overpowering. After one long journey, to Vancouver, he complained philosophically to the Mayor that he felt rather like a poached egg. But it could have been worse. At Hamilton, the train driver mistook the beginnings of the town's musical farewell to its visitors for a signal to move. The train trundled off down the line, till the mistake was realised, and the red-faced driver had to reverse it and collect his royal passengers. Little else went desperately wrong on the tour — at least until they reached Halifax, where Princess Elizabeth presented a Cup to a Mountie who had won a shooting competition. The champion first dropped the base of the Cup; then, as the Duke stooped to pick it up for him, dropped the Cup itself, complete with lid.

Incidents like these tended to obscure the serious side of the tour, but there are still plaques throughout the whole breadth of the country to prove the more earnest purpose of the royal visit. Significantly, the Princess and her husband kept Remembrance Day with the Canadians, laying a wreath at the War Memorial at St John's — just as a month earlier they had placed one at Toronto — in honour of the 42,000 Canadians who had died in an Empire's service during the recent War. The Duke occasionally struck out on

his own, as at a Board of Trade dinner in Toronto, where he praised Canadian scientists and research workers as 'second to none in the world.' For his wife, there were more domestic-orientated duties, including the presentation of a gros-point tapestry carpet, worked by Queen Mary herself, to the National Gallery in Ottawa.

Generally, however, the giving of gifts went the other way, and the royal couple came home with an abundance of presents. Jewellery was, predictably, the favourite — Quebec gave the Princess a jewelled brooch replica of the Quebec Shield, with its panel of fleurs-de-lys, while Toronto offered a gold maple-leaf brooch encrusted with diamonds. Local offerings revealed a wider range of imaginative variations, including a silver fox fur cape from Charlottetown, a bearskin rug from Edmonton, and an enormous cheese from Salmon Arm, near Kamloops. Nor were the Edinburghs' two children forgotten. Toronto gave mechanical toys for them, Windsor presented replicas of cars made by the local Ford Motor Company, Kapuskasing donated a nursery-sized radio-gramophone, while at Calgary an Indian squaw called Mrs Heavyshield presented Princess Elizabeth with a doeskin tribal suit for the 14-month-old Princess Anne. In those circumstances it was unfortunate that the royal parents could not be back in London in time to celebrate Prince Charles' third birthday in mid-November, but such are the disadvantages which go with the privilege of monumental journeys of lifetimes. By the time this one was all over, the Princess and her husband had covered over 15,000 miles in a six-week return journey which offered only brief respites, like the three-day shooting holiday at a wooden lodge at Eagle's Crest on Vancouver Island, and a snowbound weekend at Quebec. But the Princess was full of enthusiasm when she spoke of her experience, at the Guildhall on her return. Like her grandfather fifty years earlier, she hoped that 'people from the United Kingdom will continue to go out and make their life beside the fine men and women who form the nation of Canada', a country which, she said, 'is on its way to being one of the greatest in the world', and for which its people 'have placed in our hearts a love which will never grow cold, and which will always draw us back to her shores.' She was then just ten weeks away from becoming Canada's sovereign.

It was six years before the Queen returned to the

country she was to visit no fewer then fourteen times in the first 33 years of her reign, but she well remembered that last look at the Maritime Provinces as her ship sailed away in November 1951. 'When my husband and I were leaving Canada last time, in the teeth of a gale,' she told her hosts on the first day of her 1957 tour, 'we heard kindly people at Portugal Cove singing *Will Ye No' Come Back Again?* Now, after six years, I want you to know how happy I am to be in Canada once again.' The sentiment was probably more genuine than many suspected, her visit then representing something of an escape from a Britain awash with rumours about the state of her marriage, not to say some pretty incisive criticism of the monarchy and herself. Lord Altrincham had that summer claimed that 'the personality conveyed by the utterances put into her mouth is that of a priggish schoolgirl'; the playwright John Osborne had described the monarchy as 'the gold filling in the mouth of decay', and had questioned the political value and moral stimulus of 'the royal round of gracious boredom, the protocol of ancient fatuity'. Malcolm Muggeridge, famous later for jumping off bandwagons as soon as he had persuaded others to jump on, took a tilt at the Queen's 'dowdy, frumpish' appearance and 'banal' behaviour. The Queen seemed unable at first to get right away from the flak, for even as she arrived in Canada, a public opinion survey conducted just beforehand showed a marked indifference to her visit — a reaction, no doubt, to the enormous enthusiasm orchestrated and sustained at the time of the Coronation.

Nevertheless hundreds of thousands of people flocked to Ottawa give as rapturous a start to this tour as to any in the Queen's experience, and it gave her programme an initial momentum it was not to lose, despite its unoriginal format. The visit was particularly famous for the first televised broadcast ever made by the Queen — something of a trial run, one felt, for the Christmas broadcast due to be screened later that year — which was accomplished only after several long and anxious rehearsals. This was also the tour in which, at the request of Prime Minister John Diefenbaker, Prince Philip was made a Canadian Privy Councillor, and in which the Queen became the first reigning sovereign to open the Canadian Parliament in person. Persisting with the old Elizabethan theme which had been well worked in 1953, and wearing her Coronation gown for the occasion, as she had done when opening the

Australian, New-Zealand and Ceylonese Parliaments in 1953/4, she quoted the words of the first Elizabeth which, she said, were equally applicable to the second: 'Though God hath raised me high, yet this I count the glory of my Crown, that I have reigned with your love.'

The comparatively staid character of that tour contrasted sharply with the Queen's next, two years later, when the emphasis was on the need to visit many outlying districts never before visited by royalty. There was a cruise through the islands of Georgian Bay and Lake Huron, and a high-summer train journey through the Rockies; there were visits to Deer Lake in Newfoundland, to Arvida, way up the Sanguenay on Lake St John, to the gold rush area of the Klondike and to the North West Territory towns of Yellowknife and Uranium City; there were tours of aluminium-smelting plants and iron workings in Labrador and of nickel mines in Sudbury. The royal couple bumped along thirty miles of dusty road to inspect a paper mill, were invited into prefabricated homes in Schefferville, Quebec, and to workers' homes at Harmon Airbase, and met fur-trappers, fishermen and lumberjacks. 'A wonderful experience,' the Queen summed up: 'strenuous but intensely interesting. Some of the formal parts of the six-week tour were no less gruelling. There was a thirty-mile tour of Montreal's streets in boiling hot weather, while the freezing fog which greeted the Queen in Newfoundland contrasted dramatically with the 90° heat of Toronto where she was on duty for fourteen hours a day. At a Montreal ball, she and Prince Philip were forced to leave early because, as soon as they took the floor, everyone else who could crowded onto it, leaving no space for anyone to dance, while those who couldn't climbed onto chairs and tables, careless of the crash of falling cutlery and crockery around them, to get a better view of the proceedings. Officials watched helplessly as the chaos was compounded, horrified that, in the restrained words of one of them, 'the ordinary rules of behaviour were forgotten.'

The prime purpose of the royal visit was the opening of the St Lawrence Seaway, a ceremony which the Queen performed in conjunction with President Eisenhower, before she took a leisurely five-hour passage along it to the accompanying peal of riverside church bells, the blast of saluting cannon and the whistles and sirens of passing river-craft. But perhaps the visit will be best remembered for the discovery, after the event, that the Queen was then in the early stages of her third pregnancy. Although journalists had noted that, on their arrival in the country, Prince Philip looked 'subdued, in contrast to his wife's higher spirits', it was soon to be the Queen who looked increasingly off-colour as the tour continued. The strain began to tell forcibly during the western leg of the programme, though even when she missed a visit to Dawson City, the official explanation of her indisposition was given as 'a stomach upset and fatigue'. Later, 'better, but not fully recovered', the Palace warned, she completed a whistle-stop tour of fifteen townships on her journey eastwards before the final round of duties in the Maritime Provinces. It was not until she arrived back in Britain that the news of her pregnancy was released, and it is appropriate that Prince Andrew, the child born to her the following February, should have been so ·closely associated with Canada during his schooldays.

The questioning mood of the Sixties involved Canada as much as any other Western country, and the issue which raised most questions — and no little acrimony — during that decade was that of Quebec. The Queen took the full force of that debate when, in 1964, she visited Quebec as part of a short tour which also took in Ottawa and Charlottetown in celebration of the centenary of the visits of the Fathers of the Confederation. As soon as the visit had been announced, the Quebec separatists rose up in hot protest, resolved, in the words of their leader Marcel Chaput, 'to let her know brutally that she is not welcome in Quebec or French Canada.' He made veiled references to possible assassination, which others less restrained than he developed into explicit threats, and the dire possibilities developed so oppressively that the tour itself became something of a blue-print for the intense security that has surrounded the Queen ever since. She arrived at Prince Edward Island to be welcomed in a steel enclosure covered by barbed wire, massive barricades were erected everywhere, and police roamed the streets of Quebec, almost hungry for victims, on what was to become known as 'the day of the cudgel'. In the event, the protest took shape without violence, and the Queen and Prince Philip were subjected to nothing more injurious than the turned backs of thousands of separatists who lined the Quebec route, and the

virulent anti-monarchist sentiments of scores of hostile posters. From that tour, which she had long been urged to cancel for her own safety's sake, the Queen emerged almost a heroine, the subject of praiseworthy comparisons with the most dutiful and determined of her ancestors, the bold, gritty mother of four who defied the menaces of a dangerous and unpredictable foe.

After twenty years, the separatist ghost has not been laid. It raised itself in time for the Queen's Silver Jubilee visit to Canada when, despite some placatory words about the relevance of monarchy from Prince Philip in 1969, the French-speaking community collided with the federal government over the role of the Crown in Canada. Heavy debate deteriorated into such naked partisanship that, within days before the Queen's visit in October 1977, a whole consignment of Silver Jubilee memorabilia had to be destroyed because it bore English wording only, rather than English and French. The separatists' new leader, René Lévesque, worked a calculated slight to the Queen by standing in the receiving line to meet her at a formal reception, with a lighted cigarette butt clutched between his fingers. Prince Philip took the bull by the horns at a dinner party given by Prime Minister Trudeau and discussed the issue of separatism with M. Lévesque, who would only say afterwards, 'We disagreed, but subtly.' The Queen, restricted as always by protocol, could only sound a more obviously hopeful note when she addressed the Canadian people on television. 'The Canadian experience has been to illustrate that man's finer instincts can prevail,' she said, pointedly. 'My prayer is that you will continue to offer that message to mankind.'

Back in Canada the next year to open the Commonwealth Games at Edmonton, the Queen returned to the same theme, though she must by then have despaired of the state of relations between English and French-speaking communities exactly seventy years after her grandfather had pronounced them in such good order. Much of the trouble represented legacies from previous years, but in 1978 the separatists had a new grudge — that Prime Minister Trudeau might use the Queen's visit to flaunt his belief in the value of the British monarchy as presiding head of a fully federated Canada. A carefully-worded speech made by the Queen — partly in French — at St John's was translated rather too freely into pro-English sentiments, and became an immediate focus for the separatists' new protests. The matter gained such significance that the Queen herself felt obliged to put the record straight in a later speech at Regina, where she emphasised the need to draw different ethnic cultures together, rather than allowing them to flourish in isolation, or in indifference or opposition to each other. 'A free society has to be built on the co-operation and consent of all its people,' she said, 'free to enjoy and to foster the heritage of their forefathers, but at the same time willing to contribute to a distinctive Canadian culture.'

Unhappily, there was no resolution of this issue even by the time of the Queen's next visit in 1982 — the hastily-arranged, five-day stay in Ottawa to sign the Act to patriate the Constitution. There was much celebration of this long-awaited totality of independence after 115 years of diminishing reliance on Britain for constitutional status and foreign policy decisions. Mr Trudeau was jubilant — 'The end of a long winter; the beginning of a new spring,' he proclaimed — but his arch-rival, M. Lévesque, was unconvinced. 'It's crazy for the Queen to come here,' he protested. 'We refuse to accept her bringing our symbolic independence' — and he boycotted the signing ceremony, spending the day organising half-a-dozen protest meetings in Montreal and Quebec, whipping up the antipathy of the Eskimo communities who themselves had grievances over territorial claims, and encouraging all French-speaking citizens to reject the deal. The Queen faced matters squarely when she spoke at the ceremony. Referring to 'the differences and rivalries which have been part of Canada's history, and will probably always exist in such a vast and vigorous land,' she continued, 'Although we regret the absence of its Premier, it is right to associate the people of Quebec with this celebration because without them, Canada would not be what she is today.'

By then, of course, a new generation of the Royal Family had grown up, and were beginning to make their own visits to Canada. Canadians will remember with great pleasure the eventful and refreshingly informal programme assigned to Prince Charles and Princess Anne when they accompanied their parents to celebrate the centenaries of the North West Territories and Manitoba in 1970, and again — though without Prince Charles — in 1971 for British Columbia's centen-

nial. In 1978, the Queen's younger children, Prince Andrew and Prince Edward, joined her for part of that year's visit, in which the 14-year-old Prince Edward particularly enjoyed himself on a camping trip which took him along the Skyline Trial in the Rockies and during which, well protected by what appeared to be a gold-plated helmet, he toured a potash mine with his father. Two years earlier, Canada achieved something of a "first", hosting not just the Queen and Prince Philip, but all four of their children, simultaneously — the only time that all six have been together outside Britain. That was a generally happy tour, embracing as it did the formality of official duties and the homely joys of watching horses and riders at work in that year's Olympics. Having opened the Games in front of 70,000 people at Montreal, the Queen joined her family at Bromont, where Princess Anne was competing in the equestrian event. Prince Charles actually missed the opportunity to play in a couple of international polo matches in England in order to be in Canada that week but, as he explained, 'It's not every day that you can watch your sister with a chance of winning an Olympic gold.' Sadly that chance was lost. Princess Anne's horse, Goodwill, slipped in the mud, threw her and left her mildly concussed. She eventually remounted, finishing both the course and the entire event with only 24th place to show for it.

Of all the visits to Canada made by the Queen's children, surely the best and most affectionately remembered is also the most recent – that of the Prince and Princess of Wales in June 1983. It was, *par excellence*, a visit to the people, no matter how officially its programme was devised. There were, of course, buildings to open, plaques to unveil, saplings to plant and speeches to make – such are the necessary accoutrements of the royal round. But above all, the three-week progress provided an unprecedented opportunity for a conscientious yet personable Prince and his dazzlingly popular wife to make brief, informal contact with the people who comprise the nation. They graced the smallest communities with their presence, affording both adults and children the memories of a lifetime with a hand firmly shaken, a conversation snatched out of nothing, flowers and presents accepted with such surprised delight that they may have been the last thing they expected to receive on a walk-about; and for the really lucky ones, a quick kiss from the world's most adored princess. The royal couple also lent that elusive brand of distinction and purpose to the great occasion – those glittering banquets, those massive open-air parties, those national celebrations – with a combination of style and naturalness that had a lot of the less outgoing Canadian monarchists thinking again about the value of their passive indifference. Following, as it did by threee months, the Queen's own visit to western Canada, the Wales's tour made 1983 a high point in the relationship between the Crown and its Canadian subjects. Their leaders, flushed with self-congratulation in the wake the undisputed success of it all, must subsequently have come to terms with the possibility that it might be some years before another royal visit could reasonably be expected. So it was with an even greater sense of triumph and alacrity that the Canadian government was able to reveal late in 1983, that the Queen would be returning to Canada the following July, to visit the provinces of New Brunswick, Ontario and Manitoba in the course of a fortnight's tour which would constitute her fourteenth official visit as sovereign. Little did anyone imagine that the news, announced on 29th February by Prime Minister Trudeau, of his intended retirement would have anything but a superficial effect on the preparations, but when John Turner took office in the last week of June, the possibility of an early federal election emerged. Liberal ratings in the polls were high, following the attention which the media had devoted almost exclusively to Mr Trudeau's successor; the economy looked steady for the immediate future; and it was difficult to forget the stupendous victory which Mr Trudeau himself had pulled off when he took office in similar circumstances in 1968. Though a relatively unknown quantity, Mr Turner enjoyed the additional bonus of an opponent of almost equal obscurity in Mr Brian Mulroney. Against those considerations, however, was the obvious difficulty and inconvenience of knowing that, because of an anachronistic law, framed in the days of much slower communications, distancing the calling of an election from polling day itself by a minimum of fifty days, the Queen's visit would certainly have to be called off if immediate capital were to be made of the undoubted factors in Liberal favour. The alternative was to wait until after Christmas – March at the statutory latest – and risk a fall in the party's political fortunes.

The issue of the postponement of Queen's tour

resulted from the long-standing convention that she does not visit countries outside Britain during an election campaign, for fear of becoming associated with electoral partisanship – notably, of course, in the form of appearing to favour the politics of her hosts. It is a somewhat strange reservation in the case of Canada, whose Queen she is as much as she is Queen of the United Kingdom, where she continues to perform non-political duties during the prelude to elections. Indeed, Mr Turner favoured the idea of the Queen visiting Canada as one of her kingdoms, even during the campaign, provided she were kept clear of Ottawa and avoided contact with federal leaders of any political hue. But ever since early June, Buckingham Palace had warned that the Queen 'would not be in Canada during an election campaign,' and the Conservatives under Mr Mulroney were quick to make an issue of it. 'Rudely interrupt the Queen's visit,' said one, 'and then let's see what the people of Canada think.' 'It will be an outrage,' said another, 'to put off for political gain an event which has been so eagerly awaited, and on which so many people have worked for so long.'

Meanwhile the Royal Yacht *Britannia* had sailed for Canada at the beginning of July, raising hopes that a royal visit of sorts would come off – even if it meant the Queen Mother deputising for her daughter. But the prolonged official silence caused unease, frustration and eventually annoyance. In Britain, the *Daily Telegraph* ignored the fact that consultation between Ottawa and London was of daily occurrence, and imagined the Queen to have been kept totally in the dark. That clearly went too far, though there was a growing agreement with its main argument that the situation should not have reached 'the point where the Queen, who has burdens of her own, is made to appear as maid-in-witing to political opportunism. That does not dignify Canada,' a *Telegraph* leader concluded. 'It is really a matter not of politics, but of manners.' The *Telegraph* could afford its measure of righteous indignation, knowing as everyone did that Mr Turner was already packing his bags for a weekend visit to Windsor Castle to ask the Queen, in so many words, to postpone her visit. The Queen was said to have been less than pleased at the implications of his request, though that rumour was one of the more sensational interpretations of the facts. Much as she dislikes last-minute rearrangements, the Queen appreciates that governmental considerations must take priority, and she appears to have shown Mr Turner both understanding and indulgence. To have displayed, or even merely implied, impatience or bad grace would have created an unnecessary and trival constitutional crisis. Thus, 'with regret, and in the knowledge that so many Canadians have been looking forward to expressing their loyalty and affection to Her Majesty,' as the Buckingham Palace statement somewhat immodestly ran, the Queen agreed to a postponement, and Mr Turner informed his compatriots of the fact on 9th July.

With only five days before the tour would otherwise have started, there was an immediate storm of protest and dismay. It came primarily from the Conservatives, who sensed the makings of electoral victory out of what they could easily construe as a discourtesy to the Queen. Mr Mulroney predicted that his opponent 'will have to answer before the Canadian people' – a threat which Mr Turner embraced with resignation. 'If it costs me some support, then I am prepared to take it,' he countered. Other expressions of annoyance were voiced by tour organisers, one of whom angrily ridiculed the postponement 'just so a politician could win votes.' And Canon Peever, the Minister of the Trinity Anglican Church in Cornwall, Ontario, which the Queen was scheduled to visit, thought it 'disgraceful that a politician puts his own personal ambitions ahead of the needs of his peoples.'

The problems created by the postponement of the tour were enormous, as was the consequent expenditure of time, money and sheer human effort. Every town and village had its story of upheaval and disappointment, the cumulative effect of which involves mind-boggling, and possibly meaningless statistics. Perhaps the difficulties encountered by one comparatively small community – the 4,500 citizens of Prescott, Ontario – serve as a guide to the scale of the upset throughout the three provinces on the royal itinerary. Each year, Prescott stages a military pageant – the largest of its kind in Canada – recreating with prodigious accuracy the battles and strategies of what are fondly called the Loyalist Days, and the life of soldiers, camp-followers and towns-people during the troubled era between 1775 and 1815. As 1984 was not only Ontario's bicentennial year, but also the 150th anniversary of Prescott's own incorporation, the town was included in the Queen's programme, and plans for an augmented pageant made it potentially the most extensive of its kind in the whole of North America, with over a thousand volunteer participants drawn from a wide area within both Canada and the United States.

Its spectacular effect was virtually ruined by the abrupt change of plan, notified only eight days before the event, which left the organisers with the worst of all worlds. On the one hand, the outside volunteers had already irreversibly booked their annual holidays to coincide with the pageant, and the citizens of Prescott felt thus obliged to receive and host them and their families as planned. On the other hand, the whole point of the expanded celebrations was irretrievably lost because the Queen was absent when the volunteers were available, whereas when the Queen eventually arrived, at the end of September, only 200 volunteers were in a position to take part. Others were prevented by employment obligations, or by travel or accommodation difficulties. Many who could attend did so only by special arrangement with employers whereby lost time would be made up. The effect on local people extended particularly to the voluntary agencies: Prescott's St. John's Ambulance Brigade chairman, for instance, had to work evening overtime for a fortnight to compensate for time off on the day of the Queen's visit. In addition, former residents of Prescott, who had hoped to be there to see the Queen in July, simply could not alter their arrangements in order to attend in September.

The change even affected Prescott's parking facilities. The two huge fields hired to cope with buses and cars for an anticipated influx of well over 10,000 people in July had to be abandoned for fear that the traditionally rainy weather of an Ontario September might render them unusable. In its urgent search for hard standing, the organising committee was helped by Parks Canada, who offered space for 1,500 vehicles, whilst paved areas in the town were commandeered. One valuable potential parking lot near the waterfront had already been earmarked by its owners for the temporary off-loading of several thousand tons of chemical to be bought in by ship, and it was only when they generously agreed to delay the ship's arrival for a fortnight in order to make the area available, that valuable space for ninety buses was secured.

Turmoils such as this – in Prescott's case, all for a visit which would last no more than 1½ hours – were repeated throughout the three host provinces, though many organisers and the people they represented counted themselves fortunate that the events they had planned were at least capable of being staged at a later date, albeit at considerable inconvenience, not to say cost. Ontario, for instance, estimated a bill of tens of thousands of dollars for revised invitations and programmes alone; plaques which the Queen was to have unveiled had all to be recast to show new dates; the Hotel Beauséjour at Moncton, where she was due to stay, had to lay off the extra staff it had engaged, and sell at absurdly reduced prices the huge amount of extra food it had ordered – all in anticipation of a full book of reservations – and it suffered a loss of $25,000 as a result. The government of Manitoba promptly decided to send its own bill of claim direct to the federal government, who equally promptly assured the province that they had no plans for compensation. Worst hit, and most sorely disappointed, were those involved with events which could not be delayed or rescheduled – the opening of the Martin Goodman Trail in Toronto, an inter-faith service at the city's Varsity Stadium, horse-racing at the Woodbine Racetrack, the opening of Dinsdale Park at Brandon, Manitoba. And, because of prearranged duties in Cyprus and Egypt, the Duke of Edinburgh was obliged to cancel a whole sheaf of accepted invitations in Manitoba, and leave the Queen to carry out that leg of the tour by herself.

The Queen is well used to the uncertainties of life where arrangements have necessarily to be made many months in advance, and are subject to changes wrought by the vagaries of politics and diplomacy. Just now and again, she has also to contend with the perversities of the natural world, and the beginning of this tour hovered in the balance only hours before she was due to land in New Brunswick, when the area was hit by an earthquake. Fortunately, it was a relatively small one, well confined to parts outside the royal schedule, and so the Queen and Prince Philip landed, safely at last, at Moncton around lunchtime on the 24th September. Amid the familiar booming of a 21-gun salute, they were greeted by the Governor-General, Mrs. Jeanne Sauvé, by the new Prime Minister — ebulliently flushed not only with his recent political victory, but also with the pride of welcoming his sovereign within

days of a Papal visit — and by the Lieutenant-Governor and the Premier of New Brunswick.

Some seven hours before, the royal couple and their entourage of nearly three dozen had left London on a cool, airy day and under the threat of rain. Almost as if to tone with the weather, the Queen then wore a dull, bottle-green coat and matching hat whose shiny feathers flapped fiercely in a stiffish, damp breeze. With that sense of occasion which seems to inspire her to mark the first day of almost any of her Commonwealth tours with a refreshingly recent line from her wardrobe, the Queen emerged from her aircraft — a Boeing 707 supplied by the Canadian Forces — wearing a spanking new ensemble. It was an emerald green two-piece, with cheeky black polka-dot lapels, and a matching green, deep pillbox hat with a complementary polka-dot crown. The outfit's vivid *éclat* proclaimed the brighter climate into which she had flown. Here were brilliant blue skies, cloudless backdrops to the blazing reds and yellows of an Acadian fall. A summer visit might have proved warmer, but September in her best welcoming mood certainly offered compensations.

For its size — it is the third smallest of Canada's twelve provinces, and accounts for only 4% of the national population — New Brunswick boasts a diverse economy, with timber and metals heading its industrial momentum, minerals and chemicals prompting an ever-increasing mining capacity, and with the 6% of its total acreage under arable and livestock farming providing almost a tenth of its revenue. But it is not one of the Maritime Provinces for nothing, and its fisheries find cod and ocean perch, herring and tuna, crab and lobster in quantities sufficient to contribute some $300 million — or twenty per cent — to the provincial income. The little seaside resort of Shediac, just a few miles from Moncton, considers itself the lobster capital of Canada —if not of the world — and it was to that quaint, wooden-structured village that the Queen and Prince Philip travelled almost as soon as the official welcomings at Moncton were over. There was another, less formal but unashamedly proud welcome for them here as the Mayor, Michel Leger, introduced the Queen to the community's worthies, representing a population for eighty per cent of whom French is the first language. So, when the royal visitors were treated to a performance of songs by the choir of the local junior school, the repertoire consisted almost entirely of French folk-songs, reflecting the history and superbly independent culture of this unique part of the world.

The Queen was in Shediac primarily to visit its parish of St. Joseph, and to unveil a plaque at the comparatively new church — a round, modern edifice of whitewashed brick — which bears its name. It wasn't quite the oldest link with the past, because the Queen's bouquet had been received from the village's oldest inhabitant, Mrs. Leonie Williams — still lively at 102 and pleased as Punch to be at the head of the afternoon's supporting cast. Mrs. Williams was already a teenager when, in October 1901, HMS Ophir passed round the Maritime Provinces on the last leg of a voyage which had taken the future King George V and Queen Mary on an eight-month Empire tour. She still vividly remembers the day in 1939 when, like so many other Canadians, she stood at the side of a railway track, waving her Union Jack and shouting 'Vive la Reine' as King George VI and Queen Elizabeth glided by on that famous blue and silver train.

After the fetching insularity of Shediac, there was something almost cosmopolitan about Moncton, with its population of almost 60,000, where the Queen and Prince Philip returned in mid-afternoon. If they had harboured any reservations about having to leave Balmoral unusually early this year to accommodate this tour, they never showed it. Indeed, they might even have imagined that amends were being made, for at Victoria Park, as part of the civic welcome which included a walkabout among enthusiastic crowds, the royal couple were invited to watch a fine display of Highland dancing, where swords glistened, kilts flew and bagpipes blew. Nostalgic as it may have been, it was of course no more and no less than a reminder of the debt that Canadian history and culture owes to the vast Scottish influx of the last century. But perhaps it left the Queen a little less sad at having had to forego her full ten-week holiday at what Queen Victoria called 'my dearest Albert's own creation.'

With a four-hour time difference, the Queen's day had, in strict terms, already overrun when early that evening she held a brief, private audience with Prime Minister Mulroney at Moncton's Hotel Beauséjour, where she and the Duke would spend the next two nights. But the royal schedule ended there. The banquet of official welcome, which often concludes the day of arrival on tour, would provide the final flourish to the morrow, at the end of the royal visitors first full day back in Canada.

Hosted by New Brunswick's Premier, Richard Hatfield, at the Hotel Beauséjour, it was indeed a spectacular occasion. The Queen fairly glittered in her favourite, diamond-festooned tiara – a 90-year-old heirloom which Queen Mary gave to her on her marriage – and the superb early Victorian necklace of sapphires and diamonds which was a wedding present from her father, and which complementd the rich blue of her evening dress. Fanfares of trumpets seemed to herald her every move, from her arrival – a few staircases down from her suite – to her final appearance on the hotel's balcony to acknowledge the uninhibited cheers from patient and enthusiastic crowds packing the small town square below. Some said that her sparkling jewels, flashing in the floodlights, almost outdid the firework display which followed. It was understandable hyperbole, though it unfairly overlooked the enormous impact of the pyrotechnics as bursts of colour in the clear night sky accompanied the unending crackle and whizz of explosives.

The banquet itself provided the occasion for the Queen's first speech of the tour. Its theme was predictable, safe and popular, dwelling on her admiration for New Brunswick's evolution from a patchwork of ethnic communities – Indian, Acadian, French, Empire Loyalist, European – into a fully integrated and co-operative society. 'The French and the British at first fought over this land,' she recalled, 'but their descendants learned to live in harmony and to have a common purpose.' That common purpose was reflected on a large scale when the issue of Canada's constitution arose three years ago, and the Queen praised the part New Brunswick had played in preparing for its patriation in April 1982. She was pleased that, despite the two-month delay, she had at last managed to rejoice with the province on its bicentenary, and by an imaginative gesture on the part of her hosts, she was introduced to New Brunswick's first bicentennial baby. He was Daniel Val Leblanc, just nine months old and, at nine o'clock at night, only just sufficiently awake in the arms of his father Raymond to respond to what might well turn out to be the most distinguished event of his whole life.

Appropriately, that first day had taken the Queen and Prince Philip to New Brunswick's capital, Fredericton, named after King George III's second son, the Duke of York, who was born two years after the province was first colonised by British subjects. Like several other Provincial capitals, Fredericton is not New Brunswick's largest city – that honour belongs to St. John. But it is hard to beat for sheer elegance, with its charming streets lined with smart wooden houses, and its beautiful setting in thousands of acres of parkland which give it its proudly-borne nickname – 'the city of stately elms.' From a distance, there seems to rise from the intense foliage the fine, slender spire of the Victorian Gothic-styled Christ Church Cathedral, and it was there that the royal visitors had arrived late that morning to attend a service commemorating New Brunswick's bicentenary. It was a homely greeting they received from Fredericton's Archbishop and Dean, not least because the Cathedral is modelled on a 14th-century parish church in Norfolk – Sandringham country – and because it was here in 1860 that the Queen's great-grandfather, King Edward VII, discovered how similar the St. John River, beside which the Cathedral stands, was to the Thames. There was also something of an historical coincidence, though few of the churchgoers may have realised it as they nodded their approval at the Archbishop's congratulations to the Queen on the birth of Prince Harry: for it was in this very town in August 1860 that the then Prince of Wales learned by telegram of the birth of his first niece, Princess Charlotte of Prussia – the sister of the man who eventually became the Kaiser. And, to complete the nostalgia, the Queen and Prince Philip signed the Cathedral's royal bible to mark their visit – as they had done when they last called at Fredericton on a November day in 1951 so cold that they were presented with a pair of rugs emblazoned with the city's coat of arms.

The commemorative service was relayed into the nearby streets, so the congregation were not the only souls to hear Prince Philip's clear-voiced reading of one of the lessons – as he usually does on such occasions – or the Archbishop's sermonising on the distinctive contributions made to the Province's culture by a population of such varied backgrounds. This theme was well illustrated at a picnic the Queen attended at Wilmot Park that afternoon, where waving flags proclaimed the Acadian, French and British sympathies of their owners. The massive crowds gave her and the Duke a warm, effusive, yet impeccably polite welcome, highlighted by the occasional festive whoops from some of the younger contingent as the royal party arrived at the bandshell from which they viewed an hour-long entertainment by five thousand schoolchildren. It was another spectacularly bright, unseasonably hot day, and the Queen was again perfectly in tune with the weather in a delicious pink outfit and crisp white hat.

The picnic was, of course, another bicentennial celebration, and the least formal of the day. The formality came during the royal visit to the Legislative Building, where the Queen signed a warrant to create a new coat of arms to the Province – or more correctly, in the quaint wording of the warrant, to 'augment her arms in right of New Brunswick.' As you might expect of this province of bustling sea-ports, its arms are topped by a leaping fish. And, as you would certainly expect from a loyal community like this, the fish has been royally crowned. For if Fredericton is hard to match for its handsome appearance, it has few rivals in patriotism, a quality reflected in the colourful costume of the deputation of United Empire Loyalists and the Imperial Order of the Daughters of Empire, who stood at the entrance of the Legislative Building as the Queen arrived. Nine years before New Brunswick's proclamation as a province, their loyalist ancestors had fled the American Revolution, leaving Maine and Vermont for what was staunchly to remain British North America. Two centuries have not weakened the patriotic and unabashed monarchist resolve: Queen and Commonwealth are as fundamental as the very fruits of earth and sea which have made New Brunswick prosper. 'She means a great deal to all of us in Canada,' said one of Fredericton's citizens, as she waited for the Queen to arrive. 'That's why we are here.' 'She means *everything* to us,' corrected another. 'We just love her.'

That kind of admiration, a recurrent feature of the tour, became mutual when, following her final engagement in New Brunswick – a brief visit to Mount Allison University at Sackville – the Queen addressed the dignitaries and citizens of Ottawa in the afternoon of 26th September. Speaking in front of the Parliament building, she praised Canada's federal system, which she described as 'unique' and 'representing hope for the future.' To this, she added a forthright defence of the principles of parliamentary democracy which, she affirmed, 'cannot be shredded and watered down and still retain the protections and guarantees of the original. Its institutions are of a piece, supporting one another like the buttresses of a Gothic Cathedral. The lynch-pins of our freedoms must remain. In practical terms, there is no such phenomenon as a slight case of totalitarianism. Where parliamentary democracy has survived and flourished, freedom has flourished with it. When the structures of oppression are put in place, the mechanics of suppression follow.' It was the sort of speech that made you look round to see where the threat was coming from. Anyone who did found that, save for a handful of demonstrators waving a banner encouraging Western governments to 'Refuse the Cruise' there was no threat here.

Instead, Mr Mulroney, then in his tenth day as Prime Minister, spoke fulsomely of the Crown, which had 'emerged' (though from what he did not say) 'stronger and more adaptable, and indeed more relevant to the needs of a united Canada.' His words reflected the mood of the people he was addressing. Parliament Hill is no easy place to fill, but there was no shortage of enthusiasm among the crowds as the Royal Anthem struck up, and the 21-gun salute, fired from across the Ottawa River, reverberated against the walls of the imposing Victorian Gothic Parliament building. Reassuring, too, was the guard of honour, found by the Royal 22nd Regiment: not only did they afford at least a token protection, but in their familiar garb of scarlet tunics and black bearskins, they were bound to remind the Queen – like much else during this packed fortnight – of home. Nevertheless, the fact that she was in Canada's federal capital was acknowledged by her tactful choice of clothes – a vibrantly bright red coat with a red-trimmed white hat, to blend with the mass of maple-leaf flags fluttering about her. The thought was much appreciated as she and Prince Philip began their customary walkabout, gathering armfuls of flower-baskets and posies from hordes of delighted schoolchildren, both givers and receivers oblivious of the strong, cool breeze which contrasted with the sunnier climes of New Brunswick. Then out came the State landau – over a century old, pulled by four black horses

and escorted by four dozen mounted police in the rich scarlet and gold of their full ceremonial dress – and off went the royal party at a respectable trot, *en route* for Rideau Hall, the residence of the Governor-General, to meet members of the new Federal Cabinet. As befits the capital city of one of the most loyal monarchies in the world, it was an impressive domestic display of what the Prime Minister had that afternoon called 'the splendid continuity of monarchy.'

That continuity was never better illustrated than on the following day, when the Queen and Prince Philip travelled along the St. Lawrence River to visit a string of settlements which owe both origin and identity to two centuries of intense and unbroken loyalty to the Crown. It was a journey through the very roots of Upper Canada, which is dotted with towns whose founders had fled the American Revolution, and raised regiments to carry out protective raids against republican attacks across the river until well into the second decade of the nineteenth century. It was also something of a nostalgic journey, for just 25 years earlier, the Queen had joined President Eisenhower in opening the St. Lawrence Seaway. And it was along that seaway now that the Royal Yacht *Britannia* steamed a stately passage to keep pace with the royal couple's stop-go progress to call on four communities in the space of ten hours.

A detachment of Mounties had followed the Queen from Ottawa, to provide a guard as she and Prince Philip stepped ashore from the Royal Yacht to pass through Morrisburg on their way to Cornwall. Cornwall, a city of some 45,000 people, was named in honour of the Dukedom of Cornwall in 1787, but it was its incorporation in 1834 that the Queen was here to celebrate. The pure thrill of the autumnal backdrop in this most gently scenic of regions seemed to have an invigorating effect on the visitors; Prince Philip greeted Ontario's Premier, William Davis, with a brisk 'Very cold morning!' as he watched *Britannia* being sprayed by the chilly, choppy waves of the St. Lawrence, while the Queen made much of the bouquet of white flowers given to her by nine-year-old Ricky Lapierre, and tried to identify them by their scent. She herself was well wrapped up in a warm mohair coat of blue and purple, which she had also worn on a damp day in British Columbia eighteen months before. Rather less well protected was a line of First

World War veterans, who covered themselves in blankets for the long wait before her arrival at Cornwall's Civic Complex. Here, the Queen received a municipal welcome which included a greeting in English by the Mayor, one in French by the City Clerk, and a flypast by 414 Squadron of the Canadian Forces.

Then on she went to celebrate another birthday – the centenary of the consecration of the Trinity Bishop Strachan Anglican Church in Cornwall. The church prides itself on being founded on land granted directly by George III in 1819, the year before his death, and the Queen's half-hour visit included a look at parish artifacts, the stained glass windows in the Lady Chapel, a model of the original church – built fourteen years before the land was actually granted – and a tour of the churchyard to view some of its oldest gravestones. For most tourists, half an hour would not be nearly enough, but with a heavy schedule to get through, the Queen and Prince Philip had to be on their way. Their transport was a blue and grey train, commissioned in 1967, and consisting of three carriages – two normally used by the Prime Minister, and one by the Governor-General – and known as the Governor-General's train. The departure for Prescott was delayed for a few minutes, which was bad news for the bagpipers who were constrained to play *Will Ye No' Come Back Again?* for rather longer than expected, but good news for one little girl who finally found the nerve to dash across the platform, anorak flying, to present the Queen with a posy. As the royal couple were already high up on the observation platform, a policeman had to lift the toddler up so that the bunch of yellow flowers could be delivered personally, before she scooted back to her mother. Then the whole procedure was repeated at the mother's prompting, so that a photograph of daughter and monarch together could be taken for the family album. It's not quite the use to which the Queen likes to be put, but there seemed to be no hard feelings this time.

There were certainly no hard feelings at Prescott, where the Queen and Prince Philip were treated to a modern statement of affection and loyalty imaginatively wrapped up in an authentic historical package. No ordinary civic welcome awaited them here, where Fort Wellington, hard by the deep-water port, and built to prevent the severing of this part of Upper Canada by

assaults from the American side of the river, now bristled with all the paraphernalia of 19th-century warfare – halberds, bayonets, pikestaffs – as its old wooden stockade was surrounded by replica regiments of the old fighting days. Regimental names combined the aspiring with the parochial – King's Rangers stood alongside Jessup's Rangers; the King's Regiment of New York alongside the red-kilted Royal Highland Emigrants. Tricorns, plumed bucket-hats and tartan-trimmed glengarries bobbed everywhere. The place was alive with scarlet, gold, white and green, and swamped with the sound of fife and drum. Every year they gather here to recreate the tactics of the olden days, with a detail of drill and discipline that would gladden the heart of the most pedantic military historian. And on this day, as they marched past the Queen, every detail was perfect – even down to what one local commentator called the 'studied sloppiness' of the backwoodsmen who, loyal but untrained, shuffled along, ill-clad and proudly out of step with their better-drilled counterparts upfront. Ultimately, the boom of cannon signalled the start of a bayonet charge, which lost nothing of its authenticity until it was stopped abruptly at the very edges of the spectators' enclosure. The Queen, not always one to react spontaneously to such displays, and the Duke were mightily impressed, and they took home with them a painting, a book presented by seven-year-old Ian MacDonald – *King's Men: the Soldier Founders of Ontario* – and the echo of a resounding three huzzahs as the pageant came to an end.

Things were quieter at Amherstview – the last stop of the day's royal itinerary – where the Queen's first job was to open the newly-renamed Loyalist Parkway. Part of the original Highway 33, a former Indian track, and one of the oldest routes in Ontario, the Parkway's new name celebrated commitment to the future as well as a rejoicing in the past. The span of centuries was symbolised by royal cyphers on the pillars to which the entrance gates were hinged – George III's on one, and Elizabeth II's on the other. The Queen will have much appreciated the honour as she gleefully snipped through the blue ribbon with a pair of gold-plated scissors. At nearby Henderson Farm, 2,500 guests saw the royal couple tour an exhibition of two centuries of Ontario's farming history. They were reminded of the province's cottage industries when the Queen received a special bicentennial quilt, made by Doris

Bushell, the winner of a quilt-making competition run by the Agricultural Ministry. And, as if they needed further assurances of loyalty, the Queen and Prince Philip received a copy of *Loyalist She Remains* – a pictorial history of Ontario from the earliest settlements to the end of World War II. The royal entourage then moved on to the White House at Fairfield Park, a 191-year-old, timber-framed, clapboard-covered building, set in seven acres of land. It houses artifacts and documentation testifying to the area's domestic history and importance, and sports a mid-19th-century, second-floor verandah, from which the Queen and Prince Philip were able to take in the splendid early evening view over Lake Ontario.

There was nearly an upset at the Loyalist Mohawk site, where the Queen and Prince Philip arrived at the very end of the day to a traditional Indian welcome in which children and adults alike performed their shuffling tribal dances to the accompaniment of a tape recorder. The royal visitors were already an hour behind schedule, and one of the potential victims of a shortened programme was an artist, Robert G. Miller, the presentation of whose painting to the Queen by Mohawk children would not now take place. Until, that was, the wife of Mohawk Chief Earl Hill threatened to excise a children's performance from the event unless the presentation was restored to the schedule. It was; and the artist savoured the additional honour of a private word with the royal couple afterwards. Fortunately, the dispute failed to sour one of the most moving displays of loyalty of the tour. The Mohawks are proud and jealous of their affectionate ties with the British Crown, which date from pre-Loyalist days. Four of their ancestors – then living in New York State – came to Britain as long ago as 1710 to ask Queen Anne to provide Christian instruction, and returned with a promise of teachers and the means to build a chapel. The present chapel, which the Queen visited, was transferred to the Kingston area to be rebuilt on Crown land after the American Revolution had impelled the Mohawks to flee. The story of their first landing, at the Bay of Quinte, has now become an annual theatrical ritual, and it was performed again, especially for the Queen, here at Amherstview. In this re-enactment, just as in May 1784, the first birch bark canoe to come ashore was upturned and covered with a cloth to form an altar. Upon it were placed items of com-

munion silver originally given by Queen Anne, and prayers were said in thanksgiving for a safe flight from the revolution across the river. At the Queen's own request, the Mohawks – all from the Tyendinaga Reserve – sang a hymn in their own language, both men and women chanting solemnly on the banks of the St. Lawrence. In the darkness beyond glowed the lights of *Britannia*, waiting in silhouette to take the royal party aboard at the end of a long day. And, as if suddenly reminded by the sight of her home base, the Queen rose during the beatifully-intoned hymn and made her way, amid the applause of the crowds, to the royal barge. They were still singing as it struck out from the waterside and headed towards *Britannia*. It was a heartfelt, vaguely aethereal accompaniment to a short royal journey by water, and it was born of the kind of intense, unquestioning loyalty that must surely mark the event in the Queen's memory forever.

The Loyalist act is invariably difficult to follow, and it must have seemed to the planners of the Queen's tour that the time was now ripe for a rest day. The royal couple spent it on board *Britannia* – homely, secure, and cruising slowly across Lake Ontario towards Toronto, the centre-point of the Queen's operations for the next four days. The Royal Yacht made a majestic entrance into Toronto Harbour on the morning of 29th September, and another nippy morning it was, too. The Queen, well advised as always, wore another warm-looking coat, this time in a fierce yellow that almost defied the sun to emerge, but the little girl delegated to present her bouquet was not so lucky. Two-year-old Sarah Eisen's very best party dress took no account of the weather, and she stood freezing on the quayside, growing more restless, impatient, and eventually bad-tempered by the minute. But the Queen's approach soothed everything, and as if butter wouldn't melt in her mouth, she offered up her flowers with the sweetest of smiles.

Toronto was only a small military post – known locally as 'Muddy York' – two hundred years ago. Today, teeming with a population of over two millions, it is one of Canada's most cosmopolitan cities. Its British roots have been enriched with a diverse European representation – Italian, Greek, Ukrainian, Polish and Portuguese – and invigorated with the beginnings of a South American influx. Now celebrating the 150th anniversary of its incorporation, it awaited its accolade from the Queen, here for the first time in eleven years, as she bowled into Queen's Park in a State landau to receive Ontario's official welcome. With its mixture of salutes, presentations, signings, gifts and speeches, it differed little from other ceremonies of its kind. In reply to Premier William Davis' address of welcome, the Queen spoke of the enduring relationship between Ontario and the Crown, a feature symbolised at a ceremony in which she and Prince Philip planted two white pines – the province's arboreal emblem – in the Park's newly-landscaped bicentennial arboretum. There was a special moment for the Ontario Provincial Police, who were also celebrating a birthday – their 75th. Their musicians, dressed in their imposing Highland costume, provided the ceremonial bagpipe music, and presented a copy of their anniversary book to the Queen.

After a half-hour visit to attend the dedication of the Air Force Memorial at University Avenue – during which the Queen and Prince Philip met war veterans and watched a flypast by modern and heritage aircraft – the Queen returned to *Britannia* to give a private luncheon party for the Governor-General, the Prime Minister, and the Lieutenant-Governors and Premiers of the three provinces involved in this royal tour. The celebrity of the moment, however, was ex-Prime Minister Pierre Trudeau, whose two decades of conspicuous national service earned him the rare distinction of honorary membership of the Order of the Companions of Honour, and a thirty-minute audience during which the Queen presented its insignia to him. The royal couple then went their separate ways – Prince Philip to the Hilton Castle Harbour Hotel to present awards to 125 recipients who had reached the gold standard under the Duke of Edinburgh Award scheme; the Queen to visit Old Fort York – Britain's first military fort at Toronto, established in 1773, and briefly captured by the Americans forty years later. Here she met past and present serving members of four regiments, including the 'Princess Louise's' – the regiment of Canadian Argyll and Sutherland Highlanders, whose name recalls that for five years ending in 1883, the Duke of Argyll, husband of Queen Victoria's fourth daughter Louise, was Canada's Governor-General.

But without doubt the highlight of the day was the superb military tattoo held in the Queen's honour at Toronto's Exhibition Stadium that evening. Generally reckoned to have been the largest of its kind in Canada's entire history, it combined pageantry and thrills, music and fireworks on the grandest of scales. The Queen, swathed in mink against the night chill, arrived in the State landau, in which she circuited the arena before transferring to a white Army jeep to inspect the guard of honour. It all very nearly went wrong in those early stages, because the noise of the 21-gun salute startled the two leading horses as they pulled the landau: they shied, panicked and turned about-face to bring an otherwise magnificent procession to an embarrassing halt. Grooms and members of the Governor-General's Horseguard, who were on escort duty, were quick to untangle the tack, but by then other horses had become fretful, and the firing of cannon was cut short. Perhaps that gave Toronto another 'first' – the only town to have given the Queen an eight-gun salute!

Well-practised in the art of giving little away, the Queen appeared completely undisturbed by the incident, and following the inspection of the guard, she presented a new guidon to the Queen's York Rangers (1st American Regiment). These are the present-day representatives of a unit originally drawn from Loyalist soldiers and based at Fort York, the stockade which the Queen had visited earlier that day. Performed at a field altar comprising a stack of drums in the centre of a open-square honour guard, the ceremony provided a fleeting moment of solemnity amid all that military splendour. For, watched by over fifty thousand rapturously appreciative spectators, the pageant burst spectacularly into life five minutes later. Nine marching bands provided music varying from the strident to the lyrical, the pipes and drums of four regiments trilled and boomed their interludes, while the Royal Regiment of Canada provided the impressive sights and sounds of mass bands at their ceremonial best. There was a colourful, proudly nostalgic march-past of soldiers in historical costume, some bearing quaint, pioneering and patriotic names such as the Corps of Voyageurs, the Upper Canadian Rifles and the Volunteers of the Monarchist League. A display of armoured car tactics emphasised the modern-day role of the Queen's York Rangers, and vied with stunt-riders and thundering artillery demonstrations for the public's ready applause. And, as an unforgettable finale, no fewer than 13,000 militia and reserve army personnel filled the arena to join massed bands and contingents of Highland dancers before the crash and crackle of fireworks signalled an end to the entire proceedings. Perhaps, amid such memorable grandeur, it was a touch amusing that the military director of music should have conducted the singing of *Old Lang Syne*, and the sounding of the Last Post from a vantage point no more prestigious than the top of a yellow fork-lift truck!

More down-to-earth delights awaited the Queen and her husband the following morning when Toronto's Italian community staged its own royal celebrations at the Ethnocultural Festival site. A crowd of 20,000, the site's largest since the festivities which followed Italy's World Cup victory in 1982, gave the royal couple one of the most spontaneous and heartfelt welcomes of the entire tour. Representing well over a quarter of Toronto's population, these inhabitants of 'Little Italy' made it clear that they regarded the Queen very much as their own. 'It's not important that she's not Italian,' insisted one woman, and the evidence was on every street corner as shouts of 'La Regina' went up to greet her arrival. Wearing a sombre green wool coat with a mottled green and purple hat whose feathers shone in the morning sun, the Queen was given a crash course in Italian culture which included performances by two children's choirs, a display of grape-crushing, and impromptu folk songs about everything from donkeys to drunkards.

This brisk start to the day was followed by a more studious engagement — a visit to the Royal Ontario Museum. Planned to cover a quarter of a million square feet, it is already Canada's largest museum, and supports a wide range of major research projects, from archaeology to astronomy. Today's royal visit was the museum's fourth: the Duke of Connaught came here in 1914, two years after in was opened, and both the Queen Mother and Princess Alexandra visited it in the 1960's. The primary purpose of the Queen's presence was to open the Queen Elizabeth II Terrace Galleries, but she also took the opportunity to see the museum's famed Ming tomb complex — the principal feature of its superb Chinese collection — and the current exhibition *Georgian Canada*, before venturing outside to face another of those inevitable walkabouts.

It was her second walkabout of the day, and between them they illustrated contrasting aspects of royal protocol. One concerned Sylvia Alvarao, a young girl who, though almost totally blind, was determined to mark her birthday by being in the crowd as the Queen passed by. Somehow the Queen got to know of her presence and, amid the stampede of children rushing forward with flowers and gifts, and the forest of outstretched hands straining to touch her, she made a point of going over to Sylvia to wish her Happy Birthday. The other incident involved five-year-old Ryan Baillargeon, who ran up to the Queen, hopped about her, and asked to be picked up and kissed. The Queen, hands full of flowers, and momentarily embarrassed by this unusual request, declined as politely as she could, but young Ryan ran off in tears, inconsolable in the conviction that the Queen didn't like him. His mother tried to placate him with explanations, but failed. 'I don't want to see her again!' he wailed.

He seemed to be the only one who didn't. At the Maple Leaf Gardens, 16,000 people awaited the royal visitors as they arrived for an inter-faith service to mark Ontario's bicentennial. It is unlikely that the Queen and Prince Philip have ever attended an act of worship in which representatives of so many major world religions were present. There were over four dozen in all, from African Methodists to Roman Catholics, from Latvian Lutherans to the Federation of Sikhs, from Zoroastrians to Toronto Buddhists. The Anglican suffragan bishop of the city greeted the royal couple, the Salvation Army band and choir provided much of the music, and readings included tracts from the Jewish and Islamic faiths, as well as the exhortation to 'love thy neighbour' from St Matthew's gospel. This last was read by Prince Philip, whose walk to the stage for this solemn, ecumenical purpose was accompanied by the jarringly secular dazzle and fizz of flashbulbs from a battery of Press cameras.

Britannia was the centre of royal operations for the rest of the day. The Queen and Prince Philip held a Press reception on board, before welcoming Prime Minister Mulroney and his wife Mila for dinner. And this provided the opportunity for the Queen to put on her own show — the spectacle of Beating Retreat — which all her guests watched form the Yacht's decks as the Royal Marines marched to their own musical accompaniment on the quayside. The Queen is justly proud of this travelling display. It goes almost everywhere the Royal Yacht takes her. As always, she watched every movement of the parade with the practised and critical eye of the connoisseur, and in the comfortably relaxed surroundings of her own floating home. It probably explained why, in presenting the pageant to her admiring guests, she showed a degree of prolonged animation which is rarely paralleled elsewhere.

The royal couple were off on their travels again next day, 1st October, and Windsor was their first stop. Nothing could be more different from the Windsor they are used to, with its fine Norman castle nestling in the vast, wooded parklands skirting the Thames. Here is a thriving industrial town of almost 200,000, a key city of international commerce, and Canada's busiest port of entry. Standing on the Detroit River, it is almost of a piece with its American counterpart, Detroit City, with whose automotive industry it is closely allied. The two communities even share the same birthday festivities — Canada Day on 1st July and Independence Day on the 4th are nowadays merged into one big twin-city party.

Detroit was thus an avid spectator — over three thousand of its citizens crossing the river to see the Queen — as the royal couple arrived that morning at Dieppe Park. Now celebrating its own silver jubilee as Canada's longest waterfront park — it extends along no less than 1,100 feet of the river, one of the world's busiest waterways — Dieppe Park, whose magnificent rose garden emphasises the great horticultural traditions of Windsor, was named in honour of the victims of the abortive, highly controversial raid carried out under Lord Louis Mountbatten's orders in 1942, and which claimed almost a thousand Canadian lives. Several veterans were present from those days, one of whom, Patrick Logue, plucked up the courage to tell Prince Philip that he remembered him from his Navy days, long before he became Princess Elizabeth's fiancé. The Queen, meanwhile, was surrounded by children with their offerings, as the 6,000-strong crowd, boosted by the noisily appreciative American contingent and emboldened by the raucous background noise of sirens from cargo boats on the river, clamoured for her attentions. Anthems were struck up by the imaginatively-named Spirit of Windsor band and Scarlet Brigade band,

while a flypast by a World War II Spitfire followed the usual civic hospitality. The royal couple saw three industrial displays on the site before the Queen commemorated her visit by planting a silver maple tree. It was a busy morning, and perhaps the visitors did not have much time to think of Windsor, England. But nostalgia got the better of Mrs Mary Mitchell, despite the fact that she has been in Canada for all of the 75 years since she left Scotland at the age of ten. She was thrilled when Prince Philip actually stopped to speak to her. 'I will remember it to the end of my days,' she said. 'It makes me so homesick!'

After hosting them at luncheon at the Hilton International Hotel, Windsor said goodbye to the Queen and her husband as they flew to Brantford to visit the Six Nations Reserve of the Mohawk Indians. The community, one of the oldest in North America, grew out of a confederacy formed in the fourteenth century from tribes indigenous to the southern banks of the Grand River, and proved loyal allies of the British in the days when the Hurons and the French were the common enemy. One of its warriors, Joseph Brant, defied a tribal pledge of neutrality in the 1780's, and raised a force in defence of the Crown. The 675,000-acre tract of land the community received from King George III in recognition was named after him — Brantford. Today, the confederacy boasts a fully elective tribal government, and its schools perpetuate the Indian traditions, some of which the Queen now witnessed. The Six Nations' pride and joy is their Mohawk Chapel which, restored after almost three years and $230,000 was now to be dedicated by the Queen as a national historic site. Established in 1785, it is the earliest of all Ontario's Protestant chapels, and is the only royal chapel — King Edward VII bestowed the royal designation on it in 1904 — in the world belonging to a native people's organisation. The Queen saw how replete it is with reminders of its constant royal patronage. Queen Anne's communion siltverware was on display, as were the gifts of George III dating from 1786 — a royal coat of arms in solid oak, and wooden tablets bearing the gold-lettered Decalogue, Lord's Prayer and Apostles' Creed all in the Mohawk tongue — and the set of six stained glass windows, one of which, by royal permission, bears the present Queen's cypher.

'My people sacrificed everything, including our

homeland, for ties with the British monarchy,' Chief Wellington Staats reminded the Queen bluntly in a lengthy speech which he delivered wearing his fringed suede costume and fiery orange, blue and white eagle-feathered head-dress. Little seemed to have changed in the meantime. Many of the eight thousand present had waited up to six hours for this moment, and they whistled and shouted their appreciation as the Queen strolled among the pines to plant her own white pine tree marking the afternoon's visit. Indian dancers performed for her in their colourful native costume, and a group of singers — the Hamilton Indian Singers — harmonised their bicentennial song, *Celebrate, Ontario*. And ten-year-old Krisinda Johnson was delighted that, after only fifteen minutes' practice, she was able to deliver the Queen's bouquet to her without a hitch.

The flight from Windsor to Brantford had taken the Queen and Prince Philip within 75 miles of the aircraft which was at the same time taking President Reagan from Detroit, where he had hoped to mend a few political fences for the forthcoming American elections. The Queen, who met the President officially in 1982 and 1983, took the opportunity of exchanging greetings with him in mid-flight. 'I was delighted to learn that, metaphorically speaking, we were only divided today by a strip of water between our two countries, and I send you my warm good wishes,' she said. Mr Reagan replied in kind: 'Nancy and I wish you the very best, and hope that your visit will be a happy one. We are pleased that nothing more than water separates our countries, and pray it shall always be thus.'

Back in Toronto that evening, the stage belonged solely to the Canadians, as the federal government brought its royal guests to the Roy Thomson Hall for a gala evening of entertainment. Fanfares brayed as the Queen, ten minutes late in arriving, but scintillating in a sequinned grey satin gown, diamond tiara and diamond and ruby jewellery, was greeted by the Mulroneys. Almost three thousand invitees from all walks of Canadian life watched the hour-long performance, which included a respectable proportion of French-Canadian music, a smattering of house-jokes, including references to the new Prime Minister's home town of Baie Comeau, samples of ballet and opera, a twelve-year-old violinist who played part of a Bruch violin concerto, and

renderings of folk tunes and nursery rhymes on vibes and flugelhorn. The ten artistes, together with the Gala Singers, the Canadian National Ballet, the Royal Winnipeg Ballet and the Toronto Symphony, were presented to the Queen and Prince Philip after the show, and most of the audience stayed to line the royal route to the street outside, where the crowds were still waiting for another glimpse of the Queen. One spectator looked forward to seeing her for the twelfth time in twenty years — and did. 'I'm thrilled all over again,' she said.

Bright, sunny skies returned again the next day for a schedule full of activity for the Queen and Prince Philip in Toronto city. It began with a fascinating walkabout through Riverdale Park, where five thousand citizens, more than half of them schoolchildren, watched a non-stop display of local talent and inventiveness. A group of Morris dancers brought a touch of old England to the scene, while Indian native crafts on exhibition at the Council Fire stand reminded the royal visitors that they were still very much in the heart of Canada. A children's jazz group and choir provided a polished song and dance routine, and there was even a Court Jester to entertain in the way kings and queens were once wont to be entertained. The Queen, wearing a bright coat of peacock blue and wide-brimmed matching hat, didn't forget the five hundred or so senior citizens who had come to see her, and she spent much of her time talking to them, stooping to bring herself closer to those in wheelchairs.

They were possibly outnumbered by another group of veterans– the hundreds whose service in war entitled them to put on blazers and red berets to watch the Queen and Prince Philip place a wreath of chrysanthemums and cornflowers at the City's Cenotaph, in a ceremony which rededicated the memorial to the Canadian forces who died in the Second World War and in Korea. 'She gave us more respect today than the Government has for thirty years,' said one, rather bitterly. Others were delighted to be singled out by Prince Philip with the words: 'Here's another RCR!' — a reference to members of the Royal Canadian Regiment, of which he is Colonel-in-Chief. But for many, it was a time for intensely private thought, as the scarlet-and-black-clad buglers sounded Last Post and Reveille, a kilted piper played a lament, and the

Queen and Prince stood solemn and motionless at the foot of the Cenotaph.

Happier times lay ahead in the massively-proportioned Nathan Phillips Square, where Toronto's Mayor Eggleton declared in splendid rhetorical fashion, 'I welcome you back to Toronto on behalf of the royal citizens of this, the Queen's city of Ontario and Canada.' The Queen was delighted with this impressively-sounding introduction, and had her own kind words for Toronto in return — a city, she said, 'which has reason to be proud of what has been achieved in 150 years,' and whose reputation as a great city had 'as much to do with the nature of your people as with the height of your buildings, the size of your airport and the speed of your trains.' Her subsequent walk from here to the Peace Gardens was a particular treat for the students of Seneca Hill School, with whom the Queen spent many minutes chatting about the project they had been doing in connection with her visit, and for one woman who had spent a bootless two hours trying to see the Queen at the Ontario Museum two days earlier and now, after a further two hours, managed at least a glimpse. 'The wait was worth every minute,' she said.

Another four thousand people saw the Queen reach the Peace Gardens — 'an appropriate sesquicentennial project for the city,' she called it, as she unveiled the Dedication Stone. She went on to describe it as 'an ideal place for taking time out of our busy lives for reflection. It is only when man is at peace with himself that he can make an impact on the world around him.' And so the royal progress continued, interrupted as always by the torrent of flowers and presents from the city's impressionable young. The sudden plethora of local fancy foods may have reminded the Queen that lunch was, almost literally, round the corner — at the Sheraton Centre, to be precise, where 1,800 city dignitaries assembled for a meal costing $85,000 and consisting of smoked salmon, veal medallions with wild rice, and fruit parfait. And to commemorate the royal visit, the Mayor announced a $5,000 annual scholarship in public health nursing within the city.

If the Queen was already impressed by what seemed to be Toronto's great spending spree, there was yet more to raise her eyebrows. She moved on to the Convention Centre, recently con-

structed at a cost of around $100 million, and sporting a superb exhibition hall, ballroom, theatre and press conference area. The Queen was shown a graphics display demonstrating the different aspects of the centre, before unveiling a plaque to mark the official opening. Then it was on to St Michael's Hospital, newly redeveloped in part, and scheduled for a complete restructuring of many obsolescent buildings over the next few years. Meanwhile, Prince Philip had returned to *Britannia* to catch up on some committee work — meeting members of the executive body of World Wildlife Fund, Canada, and seeing a delegation of Old Boys from the days of the Duke of Edinburgh's Conference.

This quite prestigious day was concluded in apt fashion. The highlight of Ontario's bicentennial was the dinner given that evening for the Queen and Duke at the Harbour Castle Hotel. It was as enormous in scale and as sophisticated in quality and content as the Queen had no doubt come to expect. Over 2,000 people from all over the province were invited — some top tables having been procured more by influence, it seemed, than by merit or precedence — and the menu was little short of lavish. Terrine of partridge was followed by essence of pheasant with truffled quennelles; Pacific halibut steaks with salmon mousse and lobster sauce preceded a main course of filet mignon with parisienne potatoes; while for dessert the chef had concocted a cake-like confection in the shape of a crown. Canadian wines and champagne flowed like Ontario's rivers, and no fewer than three musical bands provided a soothing background accompaniment. The Queen, who had emerged from her gleaming Fleetwood Cadillac wearing the priceless Russian fringe tiara and heavy diamond jewellery over a silver gown trimmed with aquamarine lace, was piped into the banquet by a bagpiper's rendering of *Scotland The Brave*. She was in noticeably high spirits, seeming relieved that her host, Premier William Davis, made sufficient diversions from his set speech to keep the mood light and humorous. She seemed more than flattered when he explained that his choice of 1984 for the bicentenary had not met with total agreement from the more historically-minded of his colleagues. 'But when you agreed to come and help us celebrate,' he told her, 'I *knew* my sense of history had to be true!'

Having spent their second and final rest day on

board *Britannia,* the Queen and Duke of Edinburgh left Toronto for Sudbury — their last port of call in Ontario. Here they visited the absorbing, snowflake-structured Science North centre, built on, and indeed out of, a rocky eminence on the shores of Ramsay Lake. It is a brand new science research centre, with the refreshing difference that both scientists, students and the public can feel equally at home, encouraged to take part in the "hands on" experience in a wide range of activities including working mini-computers, smelting metals and even simulating earthquakes.

The royal couple arrived in a downpour of very cold rain, which prompted the appearance of the Queen's famous black umbrella, while a choir of 170 girls from the Collège Notre Dame, dressed in nothing warmer or drier than blouses and jumpers, shivered miserably as they waited to sing for her. Appropriately enough in such weather, the Queen was given a couple of wooden ducks by Sudbury's Mayor, Peter Wong, and, as if to rub salt into the wound, she and the Duke were shown television graphics indicating the state of the weather in London — several points higher in temperature than the 3° in which they had just arrived. Prince Philip's piloting experience was acknowledged when he was shown additional details of the weather at all of Britain's major airports, and both visitors saw a more disturbing project on the causes and effects of acid rain. But everyone reckoned that the real stars of the show were a three-month-old porcupine, and Quasimodo, a beaver who became so hungry that, almost as soon as the Queen set her disbelieving eyes on him, he tucked into a huge quantity of Camembert cheese.

The royal couple's own lunch was waiting for them in rather more congenial surroundings — Science North's temporary restaurant in The Cavern, cleverly constructed out of a natural fissure in the rock out of which the centre itself is built. After lunch, the Queen and her husband parted company. Prince Philip attended a Duke of Edinburgh Award Scheme ceremony at Sudbury's Theatre Centre, before visiting the Laurentian University Arboretum Pavilion, where he inspected displays devoted to his favourite subject — conservation — and saw the latest results of research into industrially damaged land. From there, he travelled to Sudbury Airport, leaving for London and more travels — this time to the

Middle East. The Queen meanwhile had left Sudbury in a blue, yellow and silver Nordair jet for Winnipeg.

It was to have been a joyful return to Manitoba, and there was plenty to make it so. The weather had improved to provide a sunny, warm afternoon, and the Queen transferred from a twenty-year-old beige-coloured Rolls Royce to an open Mercedes for the last part of her journey to the Legislative Building in the centre of Winnipeg. Crowds were so thick on the lawns outside that not a blade of grass was visible. Balloons proclaiming all manner of affectionate messages to the monarch bobbed above loyal heads. One group of proud Brownies held out a huge maple-leaf flag for the Queen to see, letting it crumple only when they needed their fingers to protect their eardrums from the blast of the gun salutes. The military was smart, precise and eminently watchable. But the shine was taken off the afternoon's proceedings. A gunman had been reported lurking nearby. The Post Office received a message that its building would be blown up as the Queen arrived in the city. Security took a hand, becoming so overwhelming at the Legislative Building that hordes of shoolchildren, thrilled to be having the afternoon off to see the Queen, found their view totally blocked by an immovable cordon of police standing shoulder to shoulder. A contingent from the Monarchist League discovered that its reserved place had been taken over, and was furious. Meanwhile, the Queen passed through the guard of honour without addressing a single soldier, rendering their briefing on how to react superfluous. It wasn't the best start to the Queen's first visit for fourteen years.

But things could only get better, and they did at the Provincial dinner given for the Queen by Premier Howard Pawley at the Westin Hotel that evening. It was by no means as sumptuous or as large as some of Toronto's offerings, but the sentiment was just as sincere. Almost four hundred distinguished guests joined the Queen, who was colourfully dressed in an organza gown with a boat-necked bodice busily patterned with flame-coloured poppies. They all heard Premier Pawley assure the Queen that, despite the changes in Manitoba's physical environment, and the growth of her cities and towns, the soubriquet *Friendly Manitoba,* as displayed on all motor licence plates, was still justified. Much of his speech dwelt upon the fact that the Queen was here to celebrate the 250 years since La Vérendrye established a trading post on the Red River, and he presented her with a gold medallion in an oak presentation box to commemorate the anniversary.

The Premier also gave the Queen a book about former royal visits to Manitoba, which she immediately took to. 'I am most grateful for this volume recording royal visits to the Province of Manitoba,' she replied. 'It will be a treasured memento of my 1984 visit to Canada's 'keystone' Province, as well as a reminder of earlier visits to Manitoba which I have delighted in making over the years. I look forward to finding in this volume the one or two threads which my family have contributed to the weave of biography which has created the tapestry of Manitoba's history.' Her ten-minute speech, delivered partly in French, praised the courage of the early traders, and stressed the need to carry on 'the stewardship which was the legacy of the pioneers.' She confessed that she had 'never ceased to be amazed at the vastness of this land' and assured her host that 'the memories of this visit will add to the rich store of affectionate reflections that the name Manitoba always calls to mind, and it will add a new chapter to the volume which you have presented to me.'

If, by Friday 5th October, the Queen had any doubts about the survival chances of Canada's cultural traditions, the events of that day would have disabused her for ever. Two of her engagements were almost indistinguishable from countless others – brief visits to the Tri-Service Memorial in Winnipeg, and to Brandon University to unveil the cornerstone of the Queen Elizabeth II Music Building – and they palled beside the blaze of colour and burst of activity that awaited her, first at Dauphin, then at the Winnipeg Arena.

It would be unenviable to choose the 'better' of the two events, so ingeniously had each been devised, and so professionally executed. Perhaps a personal choice might depend on the range of cultural awareness rather than on its intensity or level of presentation. But spontaneity has much to be said in its favour, and it seemed to be all around the Queen when, late that morning, she arrived at the Selo Ukraina Amphitheatre, a newly completed construction which will be the future permanent home of the Ukrain-

ian Festival, now established for almost two decades as a result of the sheer exuberant enthusiasm of the strong Ukrainian community in this part of the vast Canadian prairie-land.

The Queen's first encounter with their traditions came with a cavalry charge by half-a-dozen Cossack riders galloping with fearsome power over a newly harvested wheat-field towards her. Dressed in brilliant blues and reds, they carried with them tall flagpoles bearing Union Jacks, the Manitoba emblem, the Maple Leaf, and the blue and yellow flag of the Ukraine. They shuddered to a halt in front of the Queen and, in a potent statement of national integration and cultural independence, planted the staves in the ground. It was a taste of things to come.

The Queen spent a few minutes talking to the dismounted riders, before being led to a huge wickerwork throne from which she was to watch a lunch-time stage show devoted to the skills of many local cultures, but in which the Ukrainians continued to feature strongly. Scottish dancers performed a breezy Highland fling; a French family, les Guillas, sang a medley of charming French folk songs; a score of Indians, festooned in beads and bristling with feathers, danced to the incessant, rhythmic beating of drums; and the Dauphin Legion Pipers eventually played *Green Hills* to farewell the Queen at the end of the show. But the Ukrainians dominated in terms of colour and verve. The Cossacks executed impossible leg- and footwork, arms confidently folded and faces beaming; and dancers whirled and stomped their way through the peasant routines of their European homeland. It was a scene of ever-changing colour patterns; the boys garbed in snow-white shirts, heavily embroidered and crossed with saffron sashes, over bright green pants tucked into shining red boots; the girls deliciously wreathed in flowered headdresses from which ribbons of vibrant primary and secondary colours fell past their green blouses and long, coarse-woven skirts.

The Queen watched the spectacle with total absorption. She had already been presented with a bouquet of traditional Ukrainian flowers, and an equally traditional gift of bread, salt and a sheaf of wheat to symbolise prosperity. And she had been handed her lunch – a picnic basket full of delicacies like pickled cherries and mushrooms, cinnamon butterhorns, canapés of sausage and ham, smoked tongue, cheeses and fruits – though she carefully selected only a few pieces which she ate somewhat self-consciously, unable to conceal her dislike of taking food in full view of the general public. She seemed much more relaxed on her subsequent walkabout, almost mingling amongst the 4,000-strong crowd, and enjoying the family atmosphere in which security was markedly less obtrusive and jittery than at Winnipeg the previous day. And she was enchanted by the local arts and crafts displayed on the stands she passed – embroidery, baking, wood-sculpture, weaving – and broke her usual rule about receiving gifts from unofficial donors, by accepting a carved wooden model of a Voyageur from Léon Bouchard, a French-speaking carpenter with whom she herself readily conversed in his own language. He was very much gratified at that!

And Winnipeg was gratified by its own big show that evening – a multi-cultural entertainment which they called the Manitoba Festival. It was held in the city's hockey arena, and the Queen had the unusual and frankly dubious honour of sitting in what is normally the penalty box. An audience of no fewer than 17,000 was there to see both her and the performers, who represented as wide a range of ethnic backgrounds as ever a sovereign saw. It was a night of *tours de force* – the sheer hard work and concentration of native hoop dancers, the measured contrasts of a five-minute medley of Scottish tunes played by a band of 150 pipers and drummers, the exhausting acrobatics of the Rusalka Ukrainian Dance Ensemble, and the pure nerve of members of the Winnipeg Royal Ballet who indulged in some pop and jazz numbers to the ecstatic delight of the audience. Tracy Dahl sang a selection of Canadian songs, there was an attempt to re-create the old British music-hall, and this year's special anniversary prompted an irreverent spoof on the exploratory activities of the hero of the hour, La Vérendrye. The Queen was amused, interested, even indulgent, nodding benignly and applauding appreciatively. At the end of a day like this, a less gracious reaction seemed unthinkable.

The Queen's last complete day in Canada began with a gently amusing visit to the Costume Museum at Dugald, where two dozen ladies, up and about bright and early for the occasion, stood attired in samples of the very best in fashions during the century from 1835 to 1935. For Her Majesty, no stranger, even on this tour, to the occasional fashion brickbat, it was probably a relief to indulge an interest in something *really* old-fashioned, and she was much taken by the authentic and well thought out display of fox furs and cloche hats, lace-frilled dresses, bustled skirts, precariously balanced toques, and that *pièce de résistance*, the thick, woollen, Edwardian skating outfit that came complete with feathered hat and ermine stole. There is in the Royal Archives a photograph of Queen Mary digging potatoes, wearing a long skirt, day shoes and a large hat. It reminds you that the restraints of fashionable decorum were sometimes really as funny as our Edwardian skater from Manitoba would have us believe.

The gentility of the entire act, combining elegance and good behaviour so nicely, compared well with the incident later that morning, when a young man dressed in jeans and a red and white striped T-shirt vaulted a police barrier and ran up to the Queen in an attempt to take a photograph. Suddenly, all the security fears came back again: he was grabbed by a group of policemen, and taken off for questioning. No charges were preferred. The incident occurred at the University of Manitoba, where the Queen, none the worse for her experience, turned the sod for a new building, and presented awards to 23-year-old Michelle Roy and 20-year-old John Lavallee, in connection with the Special Olympics held this year for mentally handicapped competitors. Physical handicap was the subject of the Queen's next engagement – the opening of the Children's Hospital at the Health Services Centre. The basket of flowers she received was presented by Landon Klassan, a five-year-old boy who has successfully completed a two-year therapy course to overcome cancer. His immaculate turnout and impeccable presentation earned him spontaneous applause from crowds of onlookers and a warm smile of encouragement from the Queen.

The moist, cloudy atmosphere of that afternoon lent an authentic air to the ceremony that was to be the centre-piece of the Queen's programme in Winnipeg. At St Boniface – once a separate community, but now a suburb of the Manitoba capital – the Queen was taken to the Promenade Taché, which she formally inaugurated, and where La Vérendrye's arrival at Fort Maurepas in 1734 was to be re-enacted. Many people considered that the weather on this celebration day was much as it night have been at the time of his disembarkation – mysterious, unwelcoming, perhaps faintly hostile. But it was clearly not enough to discourage him, as the Queen witnessed when she turned riverward to see eight canoes advancing towards her, bearing almost a hundred men dressed in Voyageur costumes. With bagpipe music drifting eerily from their craft, they cheered themselves ashore, and the Queen went to greet them. The meeting was duly informal, the Queen being flattered perhaps by the attentions of these burly adventurers, and certainly somewhat amused by their leader, Mr Justice Monnin, who played the part of one of La Vérendrye's four sons. Complete with coyote-fur cap, he proceeded to take over as the Queen's guide, conducting her on a long walkabout flanked by huge crowds.

Unfortunately, La Vérendrye rated hardly a mention at the farewell dinner given by the Prime Minister that evening at the Winnipeg Convention Centre. His name did not even grace any of the menu's superb dishes – rainbow trout in white wine sauce, consommé "brunoise", braised duckling with orange sauce, parsleyed potatoes and haricot beans in butter, followed by Grand Marnier ice. Instead, the Prime Minister, in front of 1,800 representatives from Manitoba and the Western provinces, praised the Queen who, 'having participated in many of the major celebrations of 1984, have had an opportunity of viewing the dreams of Canadians at close range. You and Prince Philip have been models of gracious understanding, sympathetic to Canadian nationhood, and symbolic of our historical evolution as a free and independent country. You have carried out your difficult and onerous duties with a warmth and charm that have endeared you to Canadians everywhere.' He applauded the unifying effect of the monarchy and its role in keeping the Commonwealth together as a force for world peace, and concluded: 'You leave these shores with deep gratitude and universal admiration for the generous and thoughtful manner in which you constantly enhance our citizenship and help shape our national destiny.'

In reply, the Queen looked back on her fortnight's tour, which she called 'a wonderful experience. The crowds of people of all ethnic origins and denominations who gave me such a warm welcome and who came to the celebratory events, demonstrated that the Crown still has a real value, and I shall continue to fulfil my duties as Queen of Canada to the best of my abilities and in the interests of all Canadians.'

The following morning, she drove to Winnipeg's Canadian Forces Base for a quick tour of the Western Canadian Aviation Museum, and saw some of the fifty vintage aircraft, including Canada's first helicopter, in its impressive collection. Then, after an official farewell ceremony, the Queen was seen off by the Governor-General and the Primer Minister, as she mounted the steps of the much more modern aircraft which would take her to Kentucky for a private visit to see some of the world's most excellent bloodstock. Behind her were two weeks of engagements in which a sizeable tally of plaques were unveiled, trees planted, speeches made and listened to, guest books signed, bouquets received and miles travelled. But, as Prince Philip made clear after his first Canadian tour of 1951, 'I am not greatly impressed by statistics, and it does not matter how many miles we went by train, by air or by car. What is important is that we made personal contact.'

Moncton

"Two months later than planned, but better late than never!" September 24th, 1984 at last saw the Queen and Prince Philip in Canada for the fifteenth time. On this occasion the welcoming province was New Brunswick, high on bicentennial celebrations, and Moncton received the royal visitors. The ceremony of welcome followed a familiar pattern, but the unofficial antics of youngsters (above and right) lent a delightful unpredictability to it all. Julie McLean was there officially (opposite), and presented her bouquet beautifully.

Moncton

Governor-General Jeanne Sauvé was the first to greet the Queen as she landed, and became her official escort throughout the ceremony (right). The Canadian army was well represented, the Royal Canadian Regiment band striking up the Royal Anthem (left), and the Combat Training Technical Services Division providing the guard of honour which the Queen inspected with her usual practised eye (far left). Dazzling blue skies and unseasonably hot weather may have surprised everyone, but the Queen was delighted by her first view of New Brunswick for over eight years. Here were the makings of some spectacular autumn scenery, the countryside burnished with the golds, reds and yellows of a perfect Canadian fall. And, as the crowds discovered as they saw the visitors travel to Shediac (below), nothing gets a tour off to a good start quite like a broad, genuine royal smile!

Shediac, Moncton

Shediac's celebrated lobsters were out of season, so the townsfolk treated the Queen to some local entertainment instead (left). At 102, Mrs Leonie Williams (top left) offered the Queen's bouquet — an honour usually reserved for children. Then it was back to Moncton for an open-air reception at Victoria Park (above and overleaf).

Fredericton

Sunshine greeted the next day too, and leafy, loyalist Fredericton looked its pristine, sparkling best. The clash of bells drifting over its elegant streets called the faithful to prayer at Christ Church Cathedral, where two very special worshippers would head the congregation. Archbishop Nutter (far left) did the honours and, only ten days from the event, could not resist a congratulatory word to the Queen on the birth of Prince Harry. "I may say as a grandparent — and we have many grandparents in this congregation — how much we rejoice," he enthused. There was no whisper of dissent in the entire town — a reminder that loyalty and devotion to the Crown and those who represent it is almost a way of life here.

Fredericton

The stately, impressive Legislative Building (left) was the venue for the unusual public ceremony in which the Queen signed a warrant (right) to augment New Brunswick's coat of arms. To reflect its prosperous fisheries, a salmon now leaps across the shield.

Fredericton

Fredericton's Wilmot Park was a-bustle with activity that afternoon as hundreds of schoolchildren and representatives from all walks of life within the town staged a massive picnic. It included an entertainment which ended in what might well be Canada's festive hallmark — the release of countless multi-coloured balloons (right).

Fredericton

Princess Anne once said how difficult it is to take an intelligent interest in things and still wear a grin. The Queen's studious appreciation of an hour of local songs left her looking somewhat absorbed (left), though she was pleased by the display of cultural togetherness which the English, Acadian and Indian elements of the programme offered. Prince Philip (far left) took a more relaxed attitude, engaging her in some light-hearted banter (top) and making great play of one little Loyalist girl's spontaneous attention to her sovereign (right). Those with a sense of history — the Queen is certainly one — will relish the thought that the bandshell in which she sat has survived the full 124 years since the Park was opened by the Prince of Wales in 1860.

Moncton

The Hotel Beauséjour was the Queen's home during her two-day stay at Moncton, but it also became a venue of State when, at the end of her second day, she and Prince Philip attended a banquet given by New Brunswick's Premier, Richard Hatfield. The Queen, resplendent in her gorgeous family jewels and wearing the Sovereign's insignia of the Order of Canada, made no secret of her pleasure at being back. "This is an historic year for New Brunswick," she said, "and you have indeed a lot to celebrate." And she praised the successive descendants of American Loyalists, Acadians, Irish, Scots and Europeans for accepting the challenges of coexistence.

Ottawa

Ottawa rarely fails her Queen, and the military display greeting her in the national capital was a model of panache and precision. The Queen's contribution to the blaze of colour was her bright scarlet coat, which matched the uniforms around her, the red carpet on which she walked, and the striped awning under which she replied to the Prime Minister's speech of welcome.

The century-old State landau took the Queen and Duke at a leisurely pace — though with a few unexpected lurches — to Rideau Hall, the Governor General's residence. Here Canada's new Prime Minister, Brian Mulroney, sat proudly with his two-week-old Cabinet, all beaming at this early meeting with their monarch, for this historic photograph (top).

Cornwall

The royal barge (previous page) took the Queen and Prince Philip from Morrisburg's Crysler Park Marina to the Royal Yacht — their home for the next stage of the tour. The following day was a big one for Minh Duc Nguyen, eager to show off her beautiful posy (bottom left)– before presenting it to the Queen at Trinity Church, Cornwall. Canon Peever (opposite) took the royal couple on a tour of the church.

Prescott

The Queen marked her visit to Prescott, Ontario by putting her distinctive signature to its brand new Municipal Guest Book. Asking her to do so was no routine gesture of civility, for they don't come much more loyal than here, along this riparian strip which fronts the St Lawrence. The history of many Ontario towns and villages is replete with tales of Loyalist derring-do, and they keep the tradition alive in Prescott by staging, each year, a display of how they kept British North America British in those dangerous days of revolution and invasion from across the water. The Queen and Prince Philip proved willing witnesses to the special edition of this annual reconstruction as, accompanied by Mayor Sandra Lawn (top right), they experienced the noise and panoply of an eighteenth-century battlefield in the shadow of the wooden stockade that is Fort Wellington. Thousands who enjoyed the spectacle and the Queen's presence there proved that loyalty is by no means dead in Prescott.

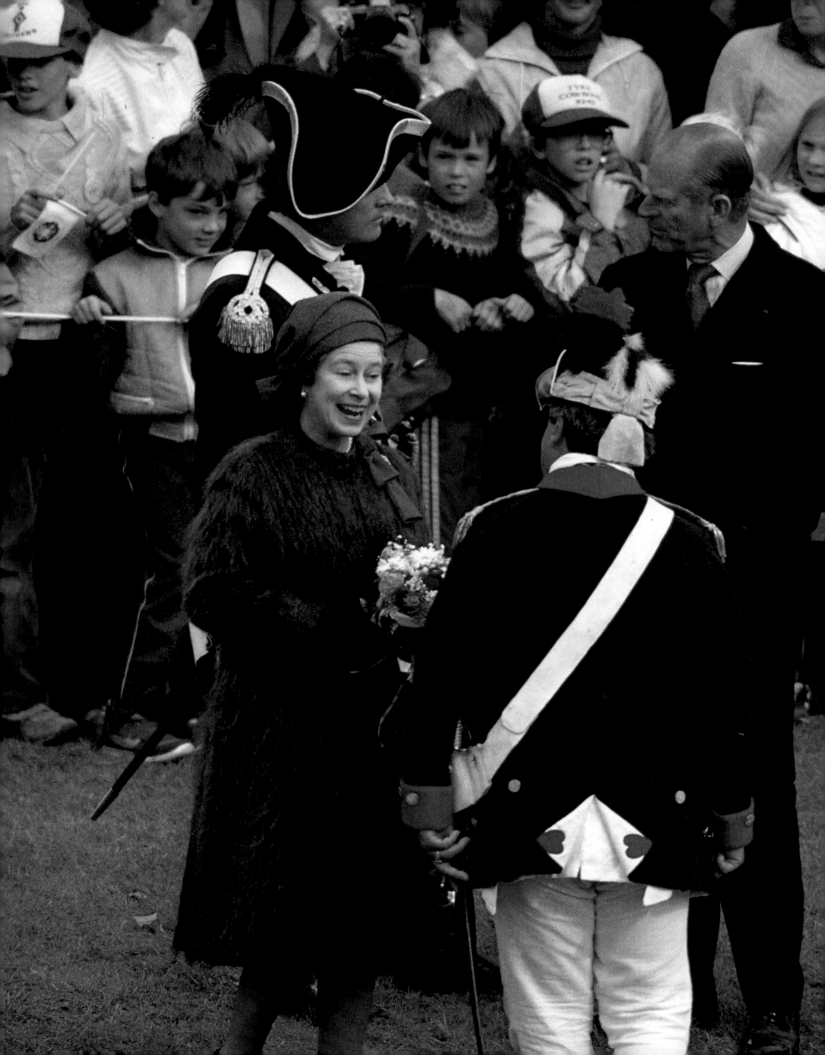

(Above) One of the five regiments whose bayonets bristled at Fort Wellington as they performed a march-past for the Queen, and (top) part of the massive crowd that watched the event. There was an element of the birthday party in all this too — Prescott was celebrating its own 150th anniversary.

Amherstview

Today's Boy Scouts (top) formed part of another fascinated audience when the Queen visited the Loyalist Mohawk site at Amherstview, where another reminder of local ethnic roots awaited her. The Indians are as proud of their traditions as anyone, and these Mohawks re-created the landing of their ancestors at the Bay of Quinte, refugees from the American Revolution seventy years after they declared their loyalty to Queen Anne. The upturned canoe (opposite, top) served as an altar for a service of thanksgiving for their safe deliverance.

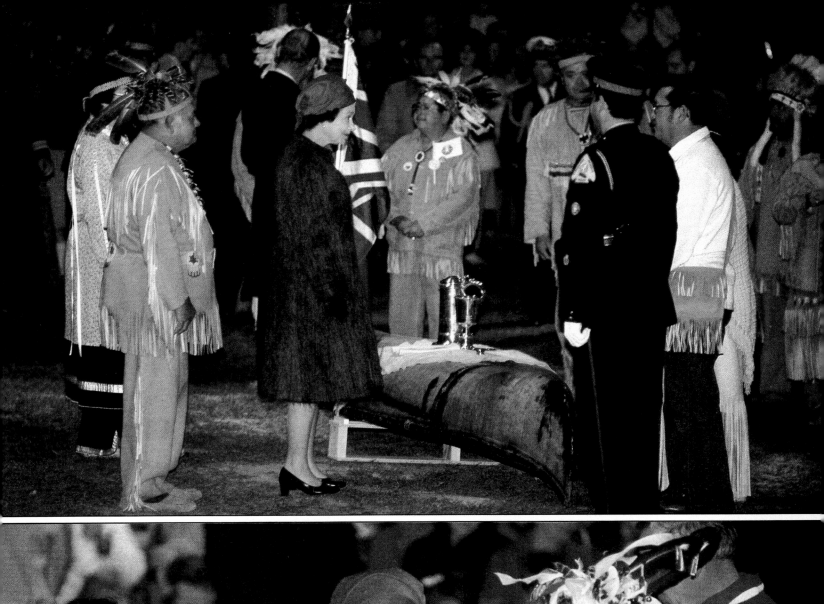

Young Sarah Eisen stole the show when she misbehaved prior to the Queen's arrival in *Britannia* (right) at Toronto, then presented her bouquet with the sweetest of smiles (opposite). "We make very

great demands of you," Ontario's Premier told the Queen at the Legislative Building. "It's a very real pleasure," she reassured him (above).

This was the Queen's first visit to Toronto for eleven years, and huge crowds turned out to watch her gleaming motorcade (top) as she travelled from Queen's Park to University Avenue. Walkabouts were very much the order of the day, though on such occasions toddlers (above) do tend to have ideas above their station…

Toronto

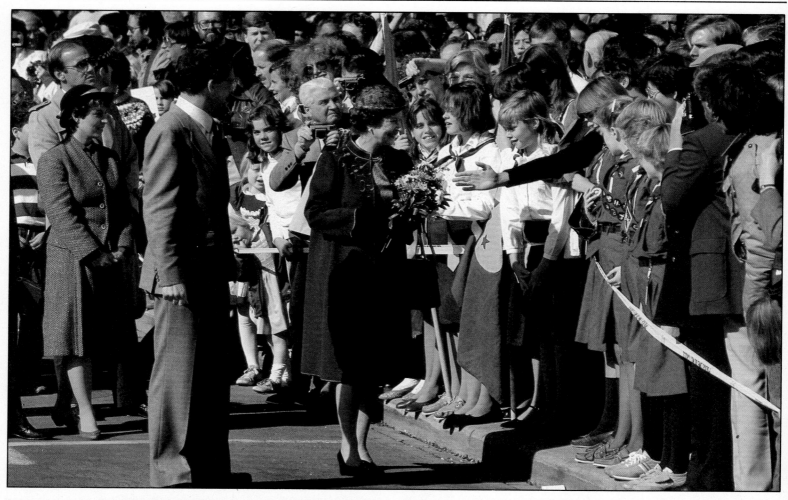

...and not just toddlers. One of the Queen's slightly older admirers (right) wanted to be picked up and kissed — but of course the Queen doesn't do that sort of thing. Perhaps he was carried away by over-enthusiasm on a morning when Toronto's vibrant Italian community pulled out all its stops to demonstrate its own special brand of admiration for La Regina. One devotee generously conceded, "It's not important that she's not Italian." Another lady spent

much of her time urging passers-by to stop and cheer the Queen. "Show some respect," she yelled. "The Queen on St Clair!" Even the district's alderman confessed himself "a little emotional", and many local churches postponed Mass so that religious fervour wouldn't conflict with royal fervour. It was a logical decision. The Italian community, now comprising over a quarter of

Toronto

Toronto's population, had campaigned long and loud for inclusion in the Queen's itinerary, and the local branch secretary of the Congress of Italian Canadians regarded her presence in "Little Italy" as a real recognition of their own presence in Canada.

Dieppe Park, Windsor was the Queen's first stop next morning, and it was eight-year-old Emily Leung's turn — supported by a couple of older companions (above), to proffer the royal bouquet. She was one of six thousand people who crowded this exquisitely landscaped waterfront, and half of them were Americans. For, as the skyscrapers of Detroit (top) made plain, the permanent, towering American presence impresses itself strongly on the good citizens of Windsor. The two communities have long regarded themselves

Windsor

as twin towns, and the common interest was much in evidence today as the more boisterous visitors from the States gave the Queen and Prince Philip a noisy, enthusiastic welcome which encouraged many Ontarians out of their natural reserve. So, too, did the special fly-past by a World War II Spitfire, which the royal couple (above) watched as part of a display staged as a tribute to those Canadians who died in the 1942 raid on Dieppe, from which the park takes its name.

The Six Nations is one of Canada's largest Indian reserves, and it was there that the Queen and Prince Philip travelled by car after landing in mid-afternoon at Brantford Airport. Chief Wellington Staats was the first to greet them, acting as host and guide throughout the thirty-minute

INTERNATIONAL
Village Queen's

Brantford

visit. The 10,000 spectators found the Queen relaxed and chatty as she strolled under the pine trees, despite a chilly wind and threatening skies. She dedicated as a National Historic Site the expensively-restored Mohawk Chapel, which provided the backdrop (top) to the ceremony of welcome, and planted her own silver pine in the chapel grounds.
The Six Nations' fierce guardianship of their traditions and culture is just the kind of thing the Queen admires — a

Brantford

virtue in itself, and a colourful contribution to the Canadian character. She will also have been gratified by the many royal associations boasted by the chapel: the land on which it stands was granted by George III, who also gifted the solid oak coat of arms and the wooden tablets engraved with the Apostles' Creed, Lord's Prayer and Ten Commandments; Queen Anne had sent out a set of Communion silver seventy years earlier; Edward VII granted it royal status in 1904, and one of the stained glass windows now bears the present Queen's cypher. Her visit emphasised the Mohawks' long relationship with the Crown, and Chief Staats asked her specifically "to continue the tradition of watchfulness over the people of the Six Nations."

Toronto

That night was very much Mr Mulroney's as he and his wife Mila hosted the Queen and Prince Philip at a glittering gala evening at Toronto's Roy Thomson Hall. It had all the makings of a State occasion — a hand-picked audience entertained by hand-picked performers, with the full might

Toronto

of the Toronto Symphony and two major ballet companies to boot. A specially-composed fanfare heralded the Queen's arrival, and in a rich, grey, satin evening dress with a busily-sequinned bodice, she sparkled in her heirloom jewellery of rubies and diamonds which complemented the blood-red of the Canadian Order pinned to her gown. The programme was delightfully mixed — with ballet performances by Evelyn Hart, Frank Augustyn and Jeff Hyslop, self-accompanied songs by guitarist Diane Tell, Guido Basso's virtuoso flugelhorn playing, and the intuitive skills of 12-year-old Corey Cerovsek on the classical violin. With probably more binoculars trained on her than on the stage, the Queen took care not to respond too spontaneously to Marie-Josée Simard's vibraphone rendering of *Pop Goes the Weasel!*

"She's important to any of us who served," said one of these veterans (opposite, below) who saw to salute the Queen rededicate Toronto's Cenotaph on 2nd October. Wearing the brilliant peacock blue outfit she wore in London the previous November to unveil Lord Mountbatten's statue, she, and Prince Philip (right) placed a huge wreath of chrysanthemum and cornflower (left) with a simple inscription (below) at the memorial.

Toronto

From the Cenotaph, the Queen took a leisurely walk to Nathan Phillips Square, stopping to chat with schoolchildren along the way (top right). One of them was pleasantly surprised to find she wasn't "a snob", while another, wearing tiara and makeshift robe, discussed her ambition to be Queen one day. The real Queen may have been surprised at Toronto's changing appearance and paid tribute to it as "a city which has reason to be proud of what has been achieved in 150 years." One such recent achievement is the Convention Centre which she visited that afternoon, taking the escalator ride (right) very much in her stride.

Truffled liver pâté, Pacific halibut steak and filet mignon were on the menu at Ontario's bicentennial dinner on the Queen's last night in Toronto. Premier William Davis' suitably respectful speech was enlivened by timely asides and the Queen was certainly tickled (bottom left) when he revealed that her agreement to visit this year settled an argument about the precise date of the anniversary.

Shortly before noon on 4th October, the Queen and Duke landed at Sudbury (top), and a motorcade (above) took them to Science North, which the Queen opened. They toured the Biosphere, Atmosphere and Geosphere areas before coming down to earth in The Cavern, where bagpipers piped them into luncheon (left and right).

Prince Philip left the Canadian tour at Sudbury, and the Queen continued the final stage on her own. It took her to Manitoba which, as its Premier was quick to point out, she had last visited all of fourteen years ago. The reminder came at a Provincial Governement dinner, and was reinforced by the Premier's gift of a book of previous royal visits to the province. "I look forward," the Queen responded, "to finding in this volume the threads which my family have contributed to the tapestry of Manitoba's history."

Dauphin

Dauphin must have rated high in the stakes to provide the Queen with the most fiery and colourful entertainment of the whole tour. Seated in a magnificent wicker chair (left) at the Selo Ukraina Amphitheatre, her bouquet of traditional Ukrainian flowers placed carefully at her feet, she watched with more than polite attention as a horsed troop of Cossacks charged at full speed towards her (opposite, top), while beribboned girls (bottom picture) sang and danced with

Dauphin

all the crisp, decorative accoutrements typical of an old-time Ukrainian village (below). A group of children offered the customary "prosperity" gifts of bread, salt and a sheaf of wheat (right), while the Cossacks proved themselves as agile on their own feet (bottom right) as they were on horseback. During all this, the Queen took a picnic lunch from a basket that had been ceremonially presented to her, but she ate sparingly, in a careful effort to balance the need for gracious behaviour towards her thoughtful and generous hosts with her well-known aversion to eating in full public view. When the entertainment was over, the Queen began a brief walkabout, meeting the

Dauphin

performers (opposite page, bottom), and visiting stands where traditional crafts (below) and domestic skills (left) were displayed. (Overleaf) The Queen attending the Manitoba Festival that evening in Winnipeg.

Dugald, Winnipeg

(Previous pages) No child admirer worth his salt ever passed up the opportunity of stepping forward to present gifts to the Queen, and the children who waited to see her at Dugald, where she saw a delightful exhibition of ladies' fashions from 1835-1935, were no exception. Later, at Winnipeg's Health Sciences Centre, the Queen opened a new children's hospital in a rather more formal ceremony (opposite).

Dugald, St. Boniface

Two of the Queen's more cultural engagements of that day — her last full day in Canada — took her to the Costume Museum at Dugald, for the parade of historical fashions (far left), and to the St Boniface site, in one of Winnipeg's suburbs, where the Voyageurs of the Red River Brigade re-enacted the arrival (left) of La Vérendrye at Fort Maurepas, near Selkirk, 250 years ago. The Queen's guide on her subsequent walk through La Vérendrye Park (opposite) was Mr Justice Michel Monnin (bottom picture), authentically dressed as one of La Vérendrye's sons.

Winnipeg

(Previous pages) Mr Mulroney greeted the Queen for the last time at the Canadian Government's farewell dinner at the Winnipeg Convention Centre — having himself arrived with his popular wife, Mila, a few minutes earlier. "I am saddened at the task of bidding you farewell," he said. "You and Prince Philip have been models of gracious understanding, sympathetic… and symbolic of our historical evolution." The compliment earned a stalwart response from the Queen: "I shall continue to fulfil my duties as Queen of Canada to the best of my abilities and in the interests of all Canadians."

At the Western Canadian Aviation Museum, the Queen saw historic aircraft (top pictures and opposite page), and met Mr Stuart McRorie (left), a former bush pilot. Then she was taken to CFB Winnipeg for a final, brief farewell from Federal and Provincial officials (overleaf) before her much more modern aircraft flew her to Lexington U.S.A. for a private visit to Kentucky's horse world.